**HIGHER**

# HISTORY
## 2006-2010

© Scottish Qualifications Authority

All rights reserved. Copying prohibited. No part of this publication may be reproduced, stored in a retrieval system, or transmitted in any form or by any means, electronic, mechanical, photocopying, recording or otherwise.

First exam published in 2006.
Published by Bright Red Publishing Ltd, 6 Stafford Street, Edinburgh EH3 7AU
tel: 0131 220 5804 fax: 0131 220 6710 info@brightredpublishing.co.uk www.brightredpublishing.co.uk

ISBN 978-1-84948-141-0

A CIP Catalogue record for this book is available from the British Library.

Bright Red Publishing is grateful to the copyright holders, as credited on the final page of the book, for permission to use their material. Every effort has been made to trace the copyright holders and to obtain their permission for the use of copyright material. Bright Red Publishing will be happy to receive information allowing us to rectify any error or omission in future editions.

907.6

£8.99

HIGHER

2006

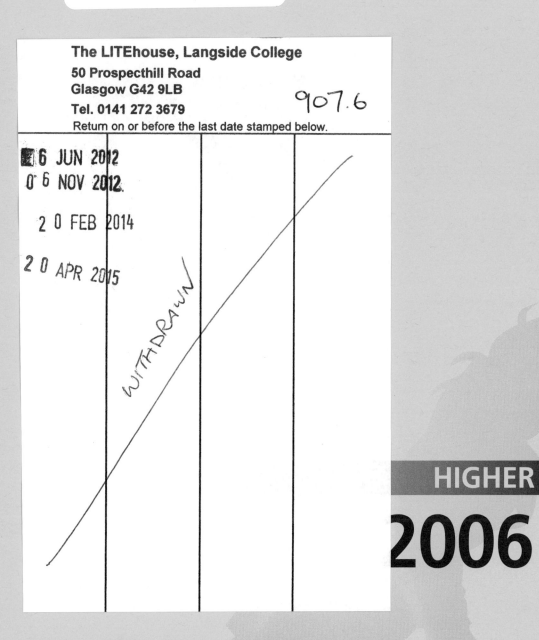

[BLANK PAGE]

# X044/301

NATIONAL
QUALIFICATIONS
2006

MONDAY, 22 MAY
9.00 AM – 10.20 AM

HISTORY
HIGHER
Paper 1

Answer questions on **one** Option only.

Take particular care to show clearly the Option chosen.  On the **front** of the answer book, **in the top right-hand corner**, write A or B or C.

Within the Option chosen, answer **two** questions, one from Historical Study:  Scottish and British and one from Historical Study:  European and World.

All questions are assigned 25 marks.

Marks may be deducted for bad spelling and bad punctuation, and for writing that is difficult to read.

SCOTTISH
QUALIFICATIONS
AUTHORITY

**[BLANK PAGE]**

## OPTION A: MEDIEVAL HISTORY

**Answer TWO questions, one from Historical Study: Scottish and British and one from Historical Study: European and World**

### Historical Study: Scottish and British

**Medieval Society**

1. How difficult were the lives of the peasants, both free and un-free, in twelfth-century Scotland and England?

2. "The medieval Church was interested mainly in secular power. Religion came a poor second." Discuss.

3. How far do you agree that towns were a vital part of medieval society?

4. To what extent was there a "Norman colonisation" of Scotland during the reign of David I?

5. Discuss the view that the quarrel between Henry II and Thomas Becket was nothing more than a clash of personalities.

### Historical Study: European and World

**EITHER**

**Nation and King**

6. "It was King John's unpleasant personality that led to the baronial opposition and Magna Carta." How far do you agree with this statement?

7. To what extent was Philip II a successful monarch?

8. To what extent did a community of the realm develop in Scotland during the period 1286–1298?

9. How important was the Battle of Bannockburn in ensuring Scottish victory in the Wars of Independence?

**OR**

**Crisis of Authority**

10. "The Hundred Years' War was fought mainly to decide whether kings of England should still hold lands in France as vassals of the French king." Discuss.

11. To what extent was the poll tax of 1380 the major cause of the Peasants' Revolt of 1381?

12. Why was the Conciliar Movement (1409–1449) unable to solve fully the problems facing the Church at the start of the fifteenth century?

13. To what extent was there a crisis of authority in Europe in the fourteenth and fifteenth centuries?

## OPTION B: EARLY MODERN HISTORY

**Answer TWO questions, one from Historical Study: Scottish and British and one from Historical Study: European and World**

### Historical Study: Scottish and British

**EITHER**

### Scotland in the Age of the Reformation 1542–1603

1. What was the most serious weakness of the Church before 1560?

2. To what extent did rivalry between England and France dominate Scottish politics between 1542 and 1560?

3. "Selfish and greedy nobles made Scotland impossible to rule." How important was this as a reason for Mary, Queen of Scots, losing her throne?

4. How important was the establishment of law and order to the success of James VI's reign in Scotland?

5. Do you consider that religious issues were the main cause of conflict in Scotland between 1542 and 1603?

**OR**

### Scotland and England in the Century of Revolutions 1603–1702

6. "Financial issues caused the most serious challenges to the authority of James I in England after 1603." How far do you agree?

7. Why did Charles I find it so difficult to rule Scotland?

8. To what extent was religion the main cause of the Civil War in England?

9. Why did Cromwell fail to find an acceptable form of government for England in the 1650s?

10. "The Glorious Revolution was the climax to the Parliamentary challenge to royal authority in the seventeenth century." Discuss.

## Historical Study: European and World

**EITHER**

**Royal Authority in 17th and 18th Century Europe**

11. How important was Louis XIV's personal role in the government of France?

12. "A disastrous failure." How accurate is this description of Louis XIV's treatment of religious minorities in France?

13. "Frederick II of Prussia was more interested in efficient government than in the welfare of his people." How far do you agree?

14. "Here lies a king who failed in all he tried to do." Was Joseph II fair to himself in writing this epitaph?

**OR**

**The French Revolution: The Emergence of the Citizen State**

15. To what extent were the grievances of the peasants a threat to the Ancien Régime?

16. Explain why the revolt of the nobles in 1787 resulted in violent revolution by 1789.

17. "The flight of Louis XVI to Varennes guaranteed the end of the monarchy." How far do you agree?

18. Why was there so much instability in France between 1793 and 1799?

**[Turn over**

## OPTION C:  LATER MODERN HISTORY

**Answer TWO questions, one from Historical Study:  Scottish and British
and one from Historical Study:  European and World**

### Historical Study:  Scottish and British

**Britain 1850s–1979**

1. Discuss the view that by 1914 Britain was not yet a democratic country.

2. To what extent did the social reforms of the Liberal Government (1906–1914) improve the lives of the British people?

3. How important were socialist societies in the growth of the Labour Party by 1906?

4. "The National Government (1931–1940) has been criticised most unfairly for its economic policies."  How far would you agree?

5. **Either**

   (a) To what extent did urbanisation benefit the people of Scotland during the period 1880–1939?

   **Or**

   (b) How far did varying levels of support for the Scottish National Party between 1945 and 1979 result from changes in the Scottish economy?

## Historical Study: European and World

**EITHER**

### The Growth of Nationalism

6. Why was unification achieved in Germany **or** Italy?

7. **Either**

   (a) To what extent was national unity a problem within Germany between 1871 and 1914?

   **Or**

   (b) What was the most serious difficulty the new Italian state faced between 1871 and 1914?

8. "Resentment towards the peace treaties at the end of the First World War made the rise of fascism inevitable." Discuss with reference to **either** Germany **or** Italy.

9. "Totalitarian rule benefited most of the people." Do you agree with this opinion about **either** Germany between 1933 and 1939 **or** Italy between 1922 and 1939?

**OR**

### The Large Scale State

*The USA*

10. How important was the Ku Klux Klan in causing the problems facing black Americans during the 1920s and 1930s?

11. Why did some Americans not share in the general economic prosperity of the 1920s?

12. How effective were the increased powers of the federal government in dealing with the social and economic problems facing the USA in the 1930s?

13. "The experience of black American soldiers during the Second World War was the main cause of increased pressure for civil rights after 1945." How far do you agree?

*Russia*

14. How important was the policy of Russification in assisting the Tsarist state to maintain its authority in the years before 1905?

15. Why did the Dumas have so little influence on the Tsarist state between 1905 and 1914?

16. "Nicholas II's fall from power was due mainly to his own weaknesses as a ruler." How far do you accept this explanation for the Revolution of February 1917?

17. How far was the failure of the White armies during the Civil War due to disunity and divided leadership?

*[END OF QUESTION PAPER]*

[X044/301]

[BLANK PAGE]

# X044/302

NATIONAL
QUALIFICATIONS
2006

MONDAY, 22 MAY
10.40 AM – 12.05 PM

HISTORY
HIGHER
Paper 2

Answer questions on only **one** Special Topic.

Take particular care to show clearly the Special Topic chosen.  On the **front** of the answer book, **in the top right-hand corner**, write the number of the Special Topic.

You are expected to use background knowledge appropriately in answering source-based questions.

Marks may be deducted for bad spelling and bad punctuation, and for writing that is difficult to read.

Some sources have been adapted or translated.

SCOTTISH
QUALIFICATIONS
AUTHORITY

[BLANK PAGE]

## OPTION A:  MEDIEVAL HISTORY

### SPECIAL TOPIC 1:  NORMAN CONQUEST AND EXPANSION 1050–1153

**Study the sources below and then answer the questions which follow.**

**Source A:** from the Bayeux Tapestry, showing the Battle of Hastings.  The wavy line under the infantry and the cavalry represents a hill.

**Source B:** from *The Anglo-Saxon Chronicle*.

William swore (before the Archbishop would place the crown on his head) that he would rule all his people as well as the best of the kings before him, if they would be loyal to him.  All the same he taxed people very severely, and then went in spring [1067] overseas to Normandy, and took with him archbishop Stigand, and Aethelnoth, abbot of Glastonbury, and Edgar and earl Edwin and earl Morcar and earl Waltheof . . . and many other good men from England.  And bishop Odo and earl William [of Hereford] stayed behind and built castles far and wide throughout this country, and distressed the wretched folk, and always after that it grew much worse.  May the end be good when God wills!

**Source C:** from the *Ecclesiastical History* of Orderic Vitalis, written *c*. 1114–1141.

When the Norman conquest had brought such grievous burdens upon the English, Bleddyn, king of the Welsh, came to the help of his uncles, bringing a great army of Welshmen with him.  After large numbers of the leading men of England and Wales had met together, a general outcry arose against the injustice and tyranny which the Normans and their comrades-in-arms had inflicted on the English.

To meet the danger the king rode to all the remote parts of his kingdom and fortified strategic sites against enemy attacks.  For the fortifications called castles by the Normans were scarcely known in the English provinces, and so the English, in spite of their courage and love of fighting, could put up only a weak resistance to their enemies.  The king built a castle at Warwick and gave it into the keeping of Henry, son of Roger of Beaumont.  After this Edwin, Morcar and their men, unwilling to face the doubtful issue of a battle, and wisely preferring peace to war, sought the king's pardon and obtained it at least in outward appearance.  Next the king built Nottingham castle and entrusted it to William Peverel.

**Source D:** from D. Bates, *William the Conqueror* (1989).

In the event of a Norman summoning an Englishman to defend himself on a serious criminal charge, such as perjury, murder or theft, a concession was made to English legal procedure. The Englishman was allowed to choose between ordeal by hot iron, which was used in England before 1066, or trial by combat, which was not. This admirably sums up William's attitude to the English: on the one hand, the ferocious crushing of all acts of violent resistance in the name of law and order, and on the other, the creation of mechanisms to resolve areas of social difference for those willing to live at peace.

For all the apparent efforts to achieve integration and reconciliation, the historian cannot overlook the fact that the Norman Conquest was a complete catastrophe as far as the English aristocracy was concerned. Many lost their lands and many more chose to emigrate in preference to living under Norman rule.

**Source E:** from H. R. Loyn, *The Norman Conquest* (1965).

William was, by reputation and in fact, one of the most active monarchs ever to have occupied the throne of England. He nevertheless remained a Norman, Duke William II of Normandy . . . William faced a very difficult political situation in the north of France . . . His main troubles came from inside his own family, especially from his eldest son Robert Curthose. Robert almost ruined the duchy, and it needed the best efforts, first of William Rufus, who held the duchy in pledge for three years when Robert was away on Crusade, and then of Henry I after his victory in 1106, to repair the damage done by their generous, irresponsible elder brother.

*[END OF SOURCES FOR SPECIAL TOPIC 1]*

## SPECIAL TOPIC 1: NORMAN CONQUEST AND EXPANSION 1050–1153

**Answer *all* of the following questions.**

*Marks*

1. How fully does **Source A** show the tactics used by Harold and William throughout the Battle of Hastings?
   *Use the source and recalled knowledge.*                                                              **6**

2. How valuable is **Source B** as evidence of William's policy towards the English immediately after the Battle of Hastings?
   *In reaching a conclusion you should refer to:*
   * *the origin and possible purpose of the source;*
   * *the content of the source;*
   * *recalled knowledge.*                                                                               **5**

3. To what extent do **Sources B** and **C** agree about the methods which William used to govern England after the conquest?
   *Compare the sources overall and in detail.*                                                          **5**

4. To what extent did William destroy Anglo-Saxon society and government?
   *Use **Sources B**, **C** and **D** and recalled knowledge.*                                          **8**

5. How effectively did Henry I deal with the problems identified in **Source E**?
   *Use the source and recalled knowledge.*                                                              **6**

**(30)**

*[END OF QUESTIONS ON SPECIAL TOPIC 1]*

## SPECIAL TOPIC 2: THE CRUSADES 1096–1204

**Study the sources below and then answer the questions which follow.**

**Source A:** an Illumination from the thirteenth-century manuscript, "Les Histoires d'Outremer", showing the Crusaders bombarding Nicea with the severed heads of captive Muslim knights.

**Source B:** from an account of the Battle of Hattin, 1187 by a local Frank, "Ernoul", written soon after 1197.

King Guy and his army left the spring of Saffuriya to go to save Tiberias. As soon as they had left the water behind, Saladin ordered his skirmishers to harass them from morning until midday. The heat was so great that they could not go on to find water. The king and all the other people were spread out and did not know what to do. They could not turn back for the losses would have been too great. He sent to the count of Tripoli, who led the advance guard, to ask advice as to what to do. He sent word that he should pitch his tent and make camp. The king gladly accepted this bad advice. Some people in the army said that if the Christians had gone on to meet the Saracens, Saladin would have been defeated.

As soon as they were encamped, Saladin ordered all his men to collect brushwood, dry grass, stubble and anything else with which they could light fires, and make barriers all round the Christians. They soon did this, and the fires burned vigorously and the smoke from the fires was great. This, together with the heat of the sun, caused them discomfort and great harm. Saladin had commanded caravans of camels loaded with water from the Sea of Tiberias to be brought up and had water pots placed near the camp. The water pots were then emptied in view of the Christians so that they should have still greater anguish through thirst, and their horses too.

**Source C:** the Massacre of Acre, from the *Itinerarium Peregrinorum et Gesta Regis Ricardi*, a contemporary chronicle of the Third Crusade, based on eye witness accounts.

Saladin had not arranged for the return of the Holy Cross. Instead, he neglected the hostages who were held as security for its return. He hoped that by using the Holy Cross he could gain much greater concessions in negotiation. Saladin meanwhile was sending gifts and messengers to the king, gaining time by false and clever words. He fulfilled none of his promises, but attempted for a long time to keep the king from making up his mind . . .

After the time limit had more than passed, King Richard thought that Saladin had hardened his heart and cared no longer about ransoming the hostages. He assembled a council of the greater men and they decided that they would wait no longer, but that they would behead the captives. They decided, however, to set apart some of the more noble men on the chance that they might be ransomed or exchanged for some other Christian captives.

He ordered that two thousand seven hundred of the vanquished Turkish hostages be led out of the city and decapitated. Without delay his assistants rushed up and quickly carried out the order. They gave heartfelt thanks, since with the approval of divine grace they were taking vengeance in kind for the death of the Christians whom these people had slaughtered.

**Source D:** from T. Jones and A. Ereira, *Crusade* (1996).

Richard was anxious to get to Jerusalem and he had no intention of hanging around in Acre for the drawn-out process of ransoming prisoners. He had nearly three thousand captured Moslems on his hands. Saladin, in his situation, would have released the prisoners. In fact Saladin had already been heavily criticised by his own people for releasing so many of the prisoners of Hattin and for allowing Tyre to be reinforced with the men he had freed.

Richard agreed with these critics. He therefore took the first opportunity of a hitch in the ransom arrangements to butcher all his prisoners. Some 2700 survivors of the Moslem garrison, with three hundred of their wives and children, were taken outside the city walls in chains and slaughtered in cold blood in the sight of Saladin's army.

**Source E:** from D. Nicolle, *The Crusades* (2001).

Before the First Crusade, most Western European states had at best a distant relationship with the Muslims of the Eastern Mediterranean. The only exceptions were some Italian merchant republics and the Norman kingdom of Southern Italy and Sicily . . . For the merchants on both sides such links were purely commercial . . . There was surely an element of economic opportunism on the part of some Italian participants in the Crusades.

The economic impact of two centuries of Crusading warfare upon some parts of Europe was considerable. In many other areas however, this impact was negligible. While in countries such as France, Germany and England the need to raise money to finance the Crusades did play some role in the development of government financial systems, it was only in Italy that the economic impact of Crusades was really important. Even here the events of the 12th and 13th centuries were only part of the longer history of the trading relationships between the Italian states and their Islamic neighbours to the south and east.

[*END OF SOURCES FOR SPECIAL TOPIC 2*]

## SPECIAL TOPIC 2: THE CRUSADES 1096–1204

**Answer *all* of the following questions.**

*Marks*

1. How useful is **Source A** as evidence of barbaric behaviour by the Crusaders?
   *In reaching a conclusion you should refer to:*
   * *the origin and possible purpose of the source;*
   * *the content of the source;*
   * *recalled knowledge.*    5

2. How fully does **Source B** describe the events of the Battle of Hattin?
   *Use the source and recalled knowledge.*    6

3. Compare the explanations for the Massacre of Acre in **Sources C** and **D**.
   *Compare the sources overall and in detail.*    5

4. How fully do **Sources B**, **C** and **E** describe the crusading ideal?
   *Use **Sources B**, **C** and **E** and recalled knowledge.*    8

5. To what extent do you agree with David Nicolle's view in **Source E** about the economic impact of the Crusades throughout Europe.
   *Use the source and recalled knowledge.*    6

(30)

[*END OF QUESTIONS ON SPECIAL TOPIC 2*]

## OPTION B: EARLY MODERN HISTORY

### SPECIAL TOPIC 3: SCOTLAND 1689–1715

**Study the sources below and then answer the questions which follow.**

**Source A:** from P. W. J. Riley, *The Union of Scotland and England* (1978).

From the parliament of 1703 emerged the Act Anent Peace and War and the Act of Security, both forced on the court by the ill-assorted opposition and both important links in the chain of events leading to the union. The first Act invested in the Scottish parliament for the future, the final decision on Scotland's declaring war. The prospect worried Godolphin but, despite his private protests to the Scottish officers of state, the queen was advised to let it become law. The Act of Security was intended to lay down the conditions under which the next successor to the Scottish throne was to be selected, conditions which would ensure that the choice was free of English influence. For the English the alarming part of the Act was the "communication of trade" clause. By this provision the separation of England and Scotland was envisaged on the death of the queen unless, in the meantime, the Scots had been granted amongst other things, full freedom of trade with England and her colonies.

**Source B:** from James Hodges, *The Rights and Interests of the Two British Monarchies* (1703).

There is a proposal for a federal union under one Monarch. In it, there shall be no other alteration in the constitutions of either Kingdom, but that each . . . are to retain their National Distinction, to enjoy their particular Liberties, Privileges, and Independence, and to hold their different governments in Church and State, with the laws, customs and rights of the same, as they did before the Union . . . This kind of union is different from that, which some insist upon for uniting the two into one kingdom, one government, one parliament etc under the title of an incorporating union . . .

A federal union is much more agreeable to the real interests of both nations . . . But it is simply impossible to consult the true interests of either nation by an incorporating union, however contrived or qualified.

**Source C:** from a speech by Seton of Pitmedden in the Scots Parliament, 1706.

There can be no sure guarantee for the observance of the articles of a federal union between two nations, where one is much superior to the other in riches, numbers of people and an extended commerce. Do the advantages of a federal union balance its disadvantages? Will the English accept a federal union, supposing it to be for the true interest of both nations? No federal union between Scotland and England is sufficient to secure the peace of this island, or fortify it against the intrigues and invasions of its foreign enemies. England should not give its trade and protection to this nation till both kingdoms are incorporated into one.

**Source D:** from Houston and Knox (eds), *The New Penguin History of Scotland* (2001).

The first vote on Article one of the Act, requiring that "the two Kingdoms of England and Scotland shall . . . be united into one Kingdom by the name of Great Britain", resulted in a crown majority of thirty-three, a comfortable but not an entirely reassuring result. The government was especially concerned about the influence of the Church of Scotland, and therefore passed a separate Act guaranteeing its Presbyterian future. This removed a good deal of popular resistance, as well as calming opposition among the Whig-Presbyterian interest in the chamber. Promises to pay off Darien investors from the Equivalent, a large lump sum of £398,085 10s sterling, persuaded Tweeddale's New Party to unite with the court. There is no question that Queensberry used the usual methods of bribery and coercion, including £20,000 sterling from the English treasury, to stiffen the resolve of government supporters who were awaiting arrears of their salaries.

**Source E:** from a letter written by the earl of Mar to the earl of Leven, 1708.

The Queen called a Cabinet Council last night, where she was pleased to call the dukes of Queensberry and Montrose, the earl of Loudon, Seafield and myself. We gave an account there of what orders the Queen had sent to Scotland, since the news of the invasion . . . It is expected that the Council will seize the horses and arms of those they think disloyal, and will also be giving their advice and instructions for securing the money, in the Mint and Bank, in case of a [hostile] landing . . . It was told to us that since both Houses had advised the Queen to arrest such persons as she had cause to suspect, and are now discussing a Bill for the suspending of Habeas Corpus Acts, it was appropriate that suspected people in Scotland should be arrested.

*[END OF SOURCES FOR SPECIAL TOPIC 3]*

### SPECIAL TOPIC 3: SCOTLAND 1689–1715

**Answer *all* of the following questions.**

*Marks*

1. How far does **Source A** explain why relations between Scotland and England were strained in the period 1689 – 1705?
   *Use the source and recalled knowledge.*    **7**

2. Compare the attitudes towards Union expressed in **Sources B** and **C**.
   *Compare the sources overall and in detail.*    **5**

3. How typical is **Source C** of the opinions of Scottish supporters of Union?
   *Use the source and recalled knowledge.*    **5**

4. How fully do **Sources A**, **C**, and **D** explain the reasons for the passing of the Treaty of Union?
   *Use **Sources A, C** and **D** and recalled knowledge.*    **8**

5. How valuable is **Source E** as evidence of immediate problems following the Union?
   *In reaching a conclusion you should refer to:*
   * *the origin and possible purpose of the source;*
   * *the content of the source;*
   * *recalled knowledge.*    **5**

   **(30)**

*[END OF QUESTIONS ON SPECIAL TOPIC 3]*

## SPECIAL TOPIC 4: THE ATLANTIC SLAVE TRADE

**Study the sources below and then answer the questions which follow.**

**Source A:** from Stephen Fuller, *Remarks on the Resolution of the West India Planters and Merchants* (1789).

In certain vast regions of the African continent, where the arts of rural cultivation are little known, the number of inhabitants grows faster than the means of sustaining them. Humane concerns force the sending of the surplus, as objects of traffic, to more enlightened, or less populous countries. These countries, standing in constant need of their labour, receive them into property, protection and employment.

**Source B:** from Peter J. Kitson, *Slavery, Abolition and Emancipation: Volume 2—The Abolition Debate* (1999).

The anti-slavery movement was made up of several different perspectives: philosophical, religious, economic, legal and political . . . In Britain many of the leading thinkers were opposed to slavery . . . Adam Smith insisted that freemen would work better than slaves and that slave labour is the most expensive form of labour . . . By the close of the eighteenth century, the slave trade was largely regarded as contrary to religion, nature and justice . . . The contribution of the Friends [Quakers] to anti-slavery opinion was vital. They believed that slavery was against the will of God as revealed in the Old and New Testaments.

Another important factor in the growth of the opposition against the slave trade was the rise in evangelical Christianity in Great Britain in the late eighteenth century, members of which increasingly came to regard slavery as contrary to the law of Christian love. The evangelical Christians combined a belief in a universal humanity with a strong sense of individual guilt as well as a desire to relieve the sufferings of people through good works.

**Source C:** from a petition to Parliament, from the Archdeaconry of Leicester, quoted in *Gentleman's Magazine LXII* (1792).

As Ministers of that Holy Religion which promotes universal love, we feel bound humbly to protest against a traffic, which is a constant violation of the most essential duties of Christianity. This, if continued under the sanction of the British Legislature, may be expected to bring down upon this country the severest judgement of Heaven.

**Source D:** from a speech in the House of Commons by Bamber Gasgoyne, 1806.

The attempts to make a popular outcry against this trade were never so conspicuous as in the late election, when the public newspapers teemed with abuse . . . and when promises were required from the different candidates that they would oppose its continuance. There never had been any question since that of parliamentary reform in which so much energy had been exerted to raise a popular prejudice . . . in every manufacturing town and borough.

Every measure that invention or skill could devise to create a popular outcry was resorted to on this occasion. The Church, the theatre and the press had laboured to create a prejudice against the Slave Trade.

**Source E:** from Adrian Hastings, "Abolitionists Black and White", in D. Northrup (ed), *The Atlantic Slave Trade* (2002).

In 1807, the bill for the abolition of the slave trade was passed by the British Parliament, just twenty years after the Abolition Committee was first formed in London. It was, despite the delay (in large part due to the counter-effect of the French Revolution and the war), an impressive achievement.

It was managed by the combination of an efficient "moderate" leadership, at once religious and political, with a nation-wide public opinion produced by a great deal of campaigning. The sustained parliamentary spokesmanship of Wilberforce, personal friend for so many years of the Prime Minister, was invaluable, though the true architects of abolition were Granville Sharp and Thomas Clarkson. A cause which in the early 1780s still seemed eccentric was rendered respectable by the underlying support of the two greatest parliamentarians of the age – Pitt and Fox. It would certainly not have been carried through without very powerful religious convictions at work. It seems hard to deny that it was due to the persevering commitment to the abolitionist cause of quite a small group of men whose separate abilities and positions were knitted together to form a lobby of exceptional effectiveness.

[*END OF SOURCES FOR SPECIAL TOPIC 4*]

### SPECIAL TOPIC 4: THE ATLANTIC SLAVE TRADE

**Answer *all* of the following questions.**

*Marks*

1. How typical is the evidence in **Source A** of the arguments used by supporters of the Slave Trade?
   *Use the source and recalled knowledge.*

   6

2. To what extent does the evidence in **Source C** support **Source B**'s assessment of the reasons for opposition to the Slave Trade?
   *Compare the sources overall and in detail.*

   4

3. How useful is **Source D** as evidence of the methods used by the abolitionists to promote their cause?
   *In reaching a conclusion you should refer to:*
   * *the origin and possible purpose of the source;*
   * *the content of the source;*
   * *recalled knowledge.*

   5

4. How fully do **Sources A**, **B** and **E** identify the issues in the debate over the Slave Trade?
   *Use **Sources A, B** and **E** and recalled knowledge.*

   8

5. How adequate is the explanation given in **Source E** for the eventual abolition of the Slave Trade in 1807?
   *Use the source and recalled knowledge.*

   7

   (30)

[*END OF QUESTIONS ON SPECIAL TOPIC 4*]

### SPECIAL TOPIC 5: THE AMERICAN REVOLUTION

**Study the sources below and then answer the questions which follow.**

**Source A:** from an article by Dr Samuel Johnson, 1774.

No man is a patriot who justifies the ridiculous claims of the Americans, or who tries to deprive the British nation of its natural and lawful authority over its own colonies (those colonies, which were settled under British protection, were constituted by a British charter and have been defended by British arms).

It is absurd to suppose, that by founding a colony, the nation established an independent power. It is equally absurd to think that when emigrants become rich they shall not contribute to their own defence unless they choose to do so and that they shall not be included in the general system of representation.

He that accepts protection, promises obedience. We have always protected the Americans. We may, therefore, subject them to government. . . . The Parliament may enact, for America, a law of capital punishment. It may, therefore, establish a method and level of taxation.

**Source B:** from a letter from Lord Barrington, Secretary at War, to Dartmouth, American Secretary, 24 December 1774.

I do not believe any ministry will ever attempt another internal tax on the North Americans by Act of Parliament. Experience has shown we do not have the strength in that part of the world to levy such taxes, against a universal opinion prevailing there that we have no right to levy them. Many among ourselves, though persuaded of the right, doubt at least the fairness of such taxations; as the Parliament knows little about the state of the colonies and as the members of neither House are to pay any part of the burden they impose.

**Source C:** from D. Higginbotham, "The War for Independence, to Saratoga", in J. Greene and J.R. Pole (eds), *A Companion to the American Revolution* (2000).

The campaign of 1776 saw Britain take the offensive; but it is hardly accurate to say that she possessed the lion's share of the advantages. Problems of transportation, communication and supply were serious concerns two hundred years ago. So were her lack of sufficient men under arms. Her generals and admirals were competent enough, though little more than that—Generals Gage, Howe and Clinton were too cautious; Burgoyne and Cornwallis were too aggressive. Admiral Howe was hesitant. Clinton called Howe's naval successors "old women" who got along poorly with their army counterparts. The British generals in America, who were Members of Parliament with alliances to rival political factions, also distrusted each other.

**Source D:** from a British Officer, describing the retreat of Washington's forces from New York, 1776.

As we go forward into the country, the rebels flee before us, and when we come back they always follow us. It's almost impossible to catch them. They will neither fight, nor totally run away, but they keep at such distance that we are always above a day's march from them. They seem to be playing at hide and seek.

**Source E:** from a letter from Lord Cornwallis to General Clinton, written at Yorktown, October 20, 1781.

Sir, I am ashamed to inform your Excellency that I have been forced to give up the posts of York and Gloucester and to surrender the troops under my command by surrendering on the 19th of this month as prisoners of war to the combined forces of America and France.

I never saw this command at Yorktown in a very favourable light . . . Only the hope of reinforcement or rescue made me attempt its defence. Otherwise I would either have tried to escape to New York by rapid marches from the Gloucester side immediately on the arrival of General Washington's troops at Williamsburgh, or I would, despite the inequality of numbers, have attacked them in the open field . . . But being assured by your Excellency's letters that every possible means would be tried by the navy and army to relieve us, I could not think myself able to attempt either of those desperate measures . . .

*[END OF SOURCES FOR SPECIAL TOPIC 5]*

## SPECIAL TOPIC 5: THE AMERICAN REVOLUTION

**Answer *all* of the following questions.**

*Marks*

1. How accurately does **Source A** identify the issues that led to the colonial challenge to British control in America?
   *Use the source and recalled knowledge.*          7

2. Compare the views expressed in **Sources A** and **B** on the question of taxing America.
   *Compare the sources overall and in detail.*          5

3. How adequately does **Source C** explain the problems faced by Britain after the outbreak of war in America?
   *Use the source and recalled knowledge.*          6

4. How useful is **Source D** as evidence of the tactics used by colonial troops in the war?
   *In reaching a conclusion you should refer to:*
   • *the origin and possible purpose of the source;*
   • *the content of the source;*
   • *recalled knowledge.*          4

5. How fully do **Sources C, D** and **E** explain the reasons for colonial victory in the war?
   *Use **Sources C, D** and **E** and recalled knowledge.*          8

(30)

*[END OF QUESTIONS ON SPECIAL TOPIC 5]*

## OPTION C: LATER MODERN HISTORY

### SPECIAL TOPIC 6: PATTERNS OF MIGRATION: SCOTLAND 1830s–1930s

**Study the sources below and then answer the questions which follow.**

**Source A:** from *Glasgow Past and Present*, 23 July 1849.

There are not less than 50,000 Irish people, or of Irish descent, in Glasgow. A very small proportion of these, as compared with Catholics, are Orangemen or Protestants. In 1846, according to information kindly supplied by the Bishop, no fewer than 3,000 children were baptised in the various Catholic places of worship in the city.

A gentleman, still living, remembers when the first Irishman planted himself down in Gorbals, where he was considered as much a curiosity for a time as if he had been a tattooed New Zealander. At the present moment the principal parts of Gorbals, in Main Street and its vicinity, are almost entirely in the possession of these invaders who, however, are generally an orderly and hard working class of people. They give little trouble to the police, as compared with their countrymen in other parts of the city. Further, Mr. R. Lindsay remembers when the first Irishman wriggled himself into the locality of Fiddlers' Close and the man was tolerated by the Scotch inhabitants by reason of his agreeing to keep the close clean.

**Source B:** from R. Swift and S. Gilley (eds), *The Irish in the Victorian City* (1985).

The Irish were thoroughly disliked and feared for the problems which they brought in their wake. Not the least of these was disease. Typhus was sometimes called "famine disease" or "Irish fever", and its association with the Irish hastened the emergence of distinct ghettoes or "Little Irelands". Some of the Irish rejected the housing standards of the native poor and were condemned for their unhygienic habits. The expectations of most immigrants were set by what was commonplace in Ireland, but Ireland was much poorer than Britain. The prominence of the Irish in the crime statistics was another cause of complaint, although their offences were mostly of a minor nature—drunkenness, petty theft and offences against the person. There were numerous complaints about the Irish share of poor relief in areas of heavy immigration . . . Indeed, many viewed the arrival of the Irish as a social disaster and residential segregation set them apart from the local population.

**Source C:** from the *Aberdeen Herald*, 4 December 1852.

The farm workers were honest, plain, hard-working men, who looked forward to the day when they or their sons would be able to get larger and larger farms as their honest savings increased. These men, in many cases, have been obliged, along with their families, to leave for our towns in order to get employment, or have emigrated to countries where their skill and hard work will be more highly appreciated. A farm servant, who may have saved fifty or sixty pounds, can not even get a small farm upon which he might invest his small sum of money. His only refuge is a foreign land; and thus it is that our very best agricultural labourers are driven from this country by the foolishness of "penny wise and pound foolish" landowners . . . It is clear that the cold and damp bothy will not persuade our young ploughmen to remain at home and give up their chance of comfort, if not wealth, in America or Australia.

**Source D:** from a statement by George Wood, a Scottish emigrant to Canada, 1842.

I emigrated to this country with my wife and five children seven years ago. We all have enjoyed good health as the climate in this part of the country is remarkably healthy. I consider that the change by emigrating here is to my advantage, and that of my family. I am quite in a different situation now in this country as regards acquired property from what I would have been in had I remained in Scotland. By adopting this country as the future home of myself and family, I am now a master, where I could never well expect otherwise than to see myself and my family as servants in the old country. The ease of acquiring property here is great, and any man, single or married, of sober, economical, hardworking and persevering habits is sure to do well.

**Source E:** from "Scotland's Story", a Scottish Television Production (1988).

The religious divide lasted well into the twentieth century. It was hard for a Catholic to make progress up the social and career ladder in certain jobs. Few Catholics obtained employment in the shipyards; the medical profession (not openly) did not encourage doctors from certain schools to enter some areas of medicine. Irish Catholics thus found things more difficult. It is fair to say however, that working class people of all faiths found progress in certain professions more difficult than middle class people.

[*END OF SOURCES FOR SPECIAL TOPIC 6*]

### SPECIAL TOPIC 6: PATTERNS OF MIGRATION: SCOTLAND 1830s–1930s

**Answer *all* of the following questions.**                                    *Marks*

1. To what extent does **Source A** reflect Scottish attitudes towards Irish immigrants in the mid-nineteenth century?
   *Use the source and recalled knowledge.*                                      6

2. How far does the evidence in **Source A** support the views of the historian in **Source B** about the impact of Irish immigration on life in Scotland?
   *Compare the sources overall and in detail.*                                  5

3. How useful is **Source C** as evidence of the reasons for Scottish emigration during the period from the 1830s to the 1930s?
   *In reaching a conclusion you should refer to:*
   * *the origin and possible purpose of the source;*
   * *the content of the source;*
   * *recalled knowledge.*                                                        5

4. How typical were the experiences of George Wood (**Source D**) of Scottish emigrants between the 1830s and 1930s?
   *Use the source and recalled knowledge.*                                      6

5. How successful were immigrant groups in being accepted as part of Scottish society between the 1830s and 1930s?
   *Use **Sources A**, **B** and **E** and recalled knowledge.*                   8

                                                                                 (30)

[*END OF QUESTIONS ON SPECIAL TOPIC 6*]

## SPECIAL TOPIC 7: APPEASEMENT AND THE ROAD TO WAR, TO 1939

**Study the sources below and then answer the questions which follow.**

**Source A:** from a letter written by a young American member of the International Brigade, 1938.

*Somewhere in Spain*

*In the event of my death, will the finder please mail this letter to my mother?*

Dear Mom

In Spain there are countless thousands of mothers like yourself who never had a fair chance in life. One day the Spanish people did something about that. They got together and elected a government that really gave some meaning to their lives. But it didn't work out the way the poor people expected. A group of bullies decided to crush and wipe out this wonderful thing the poor people had accomplished and drive them back to the old way of life.

Don't let anyone mislead you, Mom, by telling you that all this had something to do with Communism. The Hitlers and Mussolinis of this world are killing Spanish people who don't know the difference between Communism and rheumatism. And it's not to set up some Communist government, either. The only thing the Communists did here was to show the people how to fight and win what is rightfully theirs.

I was always proud and grateful that you were my Mom.

Your son

Will

**Source B:** from a speech by Winston Churchill in the House of Commons, 19 July 1937.

It is well known that ordinary guarantees for safety and order had largely lapsed in Spain, that it was not safe for people to go out at night over large areas, that murders and outrages were rife. Constitutional parliamentary government was being used . . . to cover the swift, stealthy and deadly advance of the extreme Communist or anarchist factions. They saw, according to the regular programme of Communist revolutions, the means by which they could obtain power. It was when confronted with a situation like that, that this violent explosion [the Civil War] took place in Spain.

**Source C:** from Andrew Boxer, *Appeasement* (1998).

The record of British foreign policy in this period [1930–1937] looks grim. The failure to resist aggression in Abyssinia encouraged the dictators and destroyed the credibility of the League of Nations. Italy was alienated as a potential ally. Aggression in Spain was ignored. Britain accepted Hitler's destruction of the military clauses of the Treaty of Versailles without gaining much in return. Significant differences developed between Britain and France about how to handle the dictators.

**Source D:** from a speech by Viscount Astor in Parliament, 16 March 1938.

By our failure to settle certain questions in the past we must bear a certain measure of responsibility for the way in which things have happened. By the peace treaties the Austrian-Hungarian Empire was broken up and its population divided. As a result we had economic distress in Austria. The Schuschnigg government was felt to be a weak government and there was a tendency for people to drift either to Nazis or Communists.

At present I do not believe that any government, whether democratic or totalitarian, can face the possibility of a world war. Now the long range bomber means the civilian population of Germany will suffer as much as the civilian population elsewhere. It is likely that another war will be followed by revolution and the growth of Communism. Therefore I do not think any country will consider war. I cannot help thinking the way is still open to negotiation which will lead to some all round settlement. At all events it is worth exploring. There are only two alternatives I can see. One is to talk; the other is to blind drift to war.

**Source E:** the cover of the Italian magazine, *Illustrazione del Popolo*, 9-15 October 1938.

1º OTTOBRE 1938: UNA DATA STORICA.
Le truppe liberatrici entrano nelle terre sudetiche restituite alla Germania
in virtù del Protocollo di Monaco.

The caption reads, " 1st October 1938: a historic date. The liberating troops enter the Sudetenland restored to Germany through the Munich agreement".

[*END OF SOURCES FOR SPECIAL TOPIC 7*]

### SPECIAL TOPIC 7: APPEASEMENT AND THE ROAD TO WAR, TO 1939

**Answer *all* of the following questions.**                                              *Marks*

1. How valuable is **Source A** as evidence of the motives of members of the International Brigade during the Spanish Civil War?
   *In reaching a conclusion you should refer to:*
   * *the origin and possible purpose of the source;*
   * *the content of the source;*
   * *recalled knowledge.*                                                                    **5**

2. Compare the views about the Spanish Civil War expressed in **Sources A** and **B**.
   *Compare the sources overall and in detail.*                                               **5**

3. How far do you agree with **Source C**'s assessment of British foreign policy up to 1937?
   *Use the source and recalled knowledge.*                                                   **6**

4. How typical is **Source E** of international reactions to the Munich agreement?
   *Use the source and recalled knowledge.*                                                   **6**

5. How fully do **Sources A**, **D** and **E** illustrate attitudes towards appeasement during the late 1930s?
   *Use Sources **A**, **D** and **E** and recalled knowledge.*                               **8**

[*END OF QUESTIONS ON SPECIAL TOPIC 7*]                                              **(30)**

## SPECIAL TOPIC 8: THE ORIGINS AND DEVELOPMENT OF THE COLD WAR 1945–1985

**Study the sources below and then answer the questions which follow.**

**Source A:** from a report by Simon Bourgin, an American journalist in Budapest, 5 July 1956.

The events that started in Moscow with the de-Stalinisation program have more than ever begun to have some kind of influence in Hungary—things are now moving at a pace where the results cannot be predicted . . .

On 27th June, I attended a meeting of the Petofi Club, for writers and authors. There were about 2000 people in the audience, about a third of them army officers . . .

One of the speakers was a young lady from the University of Budapest. In her speech she stated that the people in the regime had lost touch with the rank and file of the Party, and with the common people altogether. They bought their clothes and food out of special shops in Budapest, they lived in expensive five-room villas. They had forgotten that most people were crowded one family to a room, and that a lot of people in Budapest did not have enough to eat. She finished by saying that there absolutely had to be a change in Party leadership.

**Source B:** from W.R. Keylor, *The Twentieth Century World* (4th edn., 2001).

The prospect of a politically independent and militarily neutral Hungary was evidently too much for the Soviet leadership to accept. It would establish a dangerous precedent that, if followed by the other East European states, could only bring about the disintegration of the buffer zone between Russia and the West, which Russia had established after the collapse of Hitler's Reich. The "liberation" of the Soviet East European Empire and the "rollback" of Communist power to the Russian frontier suddenly seemed imminent, not because of American pressure, but because of the explosion of unrestrained nationalism in Hungary.

On 4 November 1956, the Russian Army returned in force to Budapest. The Nagy government was forcibly replaced by a puppet government under Janos Kadar, whose authority rested entirely on the presence of Soviet troops.

**Source C:** from A. Dobson and S. Marsh, *US Foreign Policy since 1945* (2001).

After the Americans discovered the Russian missiles in Cuba, there was never any argument about the fact that they had to go. They could not stay for three basic reasons . . .

First, they would have had a psychological impact which would have been very damaging politically . . . It was bad enough having a communist state in the Western hemisphere—one with nuclear weapons was just not acceptable. It would have altered the perceptions of the relative standing of the USA and the Soviet Union in the Cold War and, as Kennedy commented, perceptions contribute to reality.

Second, the missiles would have strengthened the Soviet Union's strike capability and cut down the warning time.

Third, it might have encouraged the Russians to take other chances, risking unintentional nuclear war.

**Source D:** from a policy Memorandum by Dean Rusk (Secretary of State) and Robert McNamara (Secretary of Defence) to President Kennedy, 1961.

The deteriorating situation in South Vietnam requires the attention of the United States. The loss of South Vietnam to communism would involve the transfer of a nation of 20 million people from the free world to the Communist bloc . . . We would have to face the near certainty that the rest of Southeast Asia would move closer to communism . . .

The United States should commit itself to the clear objective of preventing the fall of South Vietnam to communism . . . We must try to put the government of South Vietnam into a position to win its own war against the communist guerrillas. We should also be prepared to introduce United States combat forces if that should become necessary for success . . . It may also be necessary for United States forces to strike at the source of the aggression in North Vietnam.

**Source E:** from a speech by Senator Mike Mansfield, 1962.

If our present level of support for South Vietnam does not work, it is difficult to conceive of alternatives, with the possible exception of a truly massive commitment of American military personnel—in short, going to war ourselves against the guerrillas.

That is an alternative which I most emphatically do not recommend. On the contrary, it seems to me most essential that we make it crystal clear to South Vietnam that, while we will go to great lengths to help, the primary responsibility rests with the Vietnamese. It is their country, their future which is most at stake, not ours. To ignore that reality will not only be immensely costly in terms of American lives and resources, but it may also draw us into a conflict which we cannot win.

*[END OF SOURCES FOR SPECIAL TOPIC 8]*

**SPECIAL TOPIC 8: THE ORIGINS AND DEVELOPMENT OF THE COLD WAR 1945–1985**

**Answer *all* of the following questions.**

*Marks*

1. How valuable is **Source A** as evidence of the growth of discontent in Hungary in 1956?
   *In reaching a conclusion you should refer to:*
   * *the origin and possible purpose of the source;*
   * *the content of the source;*
   * *recalled knowledge.*            5

2. How fully does **Source B** explain the reasons for the actions taken by the USSR in Hungary in 1956?
   *Use the source and recalled knowledge.*            6

3. To what extent do the views expressed in **Source C** explain American concerns and actions over Cuba in 1962?
   *Use the source and recalled knowledge.*            6

4. Compare the views in **Sources D** and **E** on the case for American military involvement in Vietnam.
   *Compare the sources overall and in detail.*            5

5. How adequately do **Sources B**, **C** and **D** explain the reasons for tension between the Superpowers up to the mid-1960s?
   *Use **Sources B**, **C** and **D** and recalled knowledge.*            8

            (30)

*[END OF QUESTIONS ON SPECIAL TOPIC 8]*

## SPECIAL TOPIC 9: IRELAND 1900–1985: A DIVIDED IDENTITY

**Study the sources below and then answer the questions which follow.**

**Source A:** from a speech by John Redmond in the House of Commons, 15 September 1914.

For the first time . . . Ireland in this war feels her interests are precisely the same as yours. She feels that British democracy has kept faith with her . . . The men of Ireland will spring to your aid in this war.

I have promised publicly, on hundreds of platforms during the last few years, that when the rights of Ireland were accepted by the democracy of England, then Ireland would become the strongest arm in the defence of the Empire.

I would feel personally dishonoured if I did not say to my fellow-countrymen that it is their duty, and should be their honour, to take their place in the firing line in this contest.

**Source B:** from an article by Arthur Griffith in *Sinn Féin* newspaper, 8 August 1914.

Ireland is not at war with Germany. She has no quarrel with any Continental power. England is at war with Germany, and Mr. Redmond has offered England the services of the Irish Volunteers to "defend Ireland". What has Ireland to defend, and whom has she to defend it against?

There is no European power waging war against the people of Ireland. There are two European powers at war with the people who dominate Ireland from Dublin Castle.

Our duty is not in doubt. We are Irish Nationalists and the only duty we can have is to stand for Ireland's interests, irrespective of the interests of England or Germany or any other foreign country.

**Source C:** from an article in the *Irish Times*, 1 May 1916.

It is believed that most of the leaders of the Rising are dead or captured. So ends the criminal adventure of the men who declared that they were "striking in full confidence of victory" and that they would be supported by "gallant allies in Europe".

The gallant allies' only gift to them was an Irish renegade [Roger Casement]. Ireland has been saved from shame and ruin, and the whole Empire from a serious danger. Where our politicians failed, the British army has won the day.

Treason must be rooted out of Ireland once and for all. The violence and bloodshed of the past week must be finished with a severity which will make any repetition of them impossible for generations to come.

**Source D:** from F.S.L. Lyons, "The Rising and After", in W.E. Vaughan (ed.), *A New History of Ireland* (1996).

The initial unpopularity of the Rising should have been regarded by the British government as a priceless asset. This indeed it would have been, if it had not been squandered in part, by the policy of internment. This herded innocent men and women into camps alongside dedicated revolutionaries, and exposed them to a process of indoctrination of which the full consequences were only to be seen in the years that lay ahead.

In addition, the asset of public hostility to the Rising was squandered by the policy adopted towards its leaders. Not only were they tried by secret courts martial, but the executions were spun out over ten days. This was sufficient time for feelings of compassion for the victims and anger against the authorities to replace the original public condemnation of the Rising.

**Source E:** from J. Smith, *Britain and Ireland: From Home Rule to Independence* (2000).

The Anglo-Irish War was little more than a dirty war between hard men and gangsters on both sides—men who were incapable of adjusting to the normalities of peace, after the bloodletting of the Great War. It was a conflict characterised by spies and informers, of midnight executions, and a bullet in the back of the head—of guilt by association or family or religion, and of widespread intimidation of ordinary people by both sides.

Yet, it was a war neither side could win. As the reality of this sunk in by the summer of 1921, the British moved haltingly towards truce, which was formally agreed on 11 July, and opened the way to more formal peace negotiations.

*[END OF SOURCES FOR SPECIAL TOPIC 9]*

### SPECIAL TOPIC 9: IRELAND 1900–1985: A DIVIDED IDENTITY

**Answer *all* of the following questions.**

*Marks*

1. How reliable is **Source A** as evidence of Irish attitudes towards supporting Britain in the First World War?
   *In reaching a conclusion you should refer to:*
   * *the origin and possible purpose of the source;*
   * *the content of the source;*
   * *recalled knowledge.*                                                                                      5

2. Compare the attitudes in **Sources A** and **B** on Irish support for Britain in the First World War.
   *Compare the sources overall and in detail.*                                                                 5

3. How fully does **Source C** illustrate Irish reactions to the Easter Rising?
   *Use the source and recalled knowledge.*                                                                     6

4. To what extent does **Source D** explain the effects of the Easter Rising on Ireland up to 1921?
   *Use the source and recalled knowledge.*                                                                     6

5. Why was it so difficult to achieve a peaceful settlement in Ireland in the period after 1914?
   *Use **Sources B**, **D** and **E** and recalled knowledge.*                                                 8

                                                                                                              (30)

*[END OF QUESTIONS ON SPECIAL TOPIC 9]*

*[END OF QUESTION PAPER]*

[BLANK PAGE]

HIGHER

2007

[BLANK PAGE]

# X044/301

NATIONAL
QUALIFICATIONS
2007

FRIDAY, 18 MAY
9.00 AM – 10.20 AM

HISTORY
HIGHER
Paper 1

Answer questions on **one** Option only.

Take particular care to show clearly the Option chosen. On the **front** of the answer book, **in the top right-hand corner**, write A or B or C.

Within the Option chosen, answer **two** questions, one from Historical Study: Scottish and British and one from Historical Study: European and World.

All questions are assigned 25 marks.

Marks may be deducted for bad spelling and bad punctuation, and for writing that is difficult to read.

SCOTTISH
QUALIFICATIONS
AUTHORITY

**[BLANK PAGE]**

## OPTION A: MEDIEVAL HISTORY

**Answer TWO questions, one from Historical Study: Scottish and British and one from Historical Study: European and World**

### Historical Study: Scottish and British

**Medieval Society**

1. "Kings and barons received all of the benefits from the feudal system while peasants received none." Discuss.

2. To what extent was the medieval Church the most significant influence in people's everyday lives?

3. How important was the desire for protection in the development of towns in England and Scotland?

4. "David I was responsible for transforming Scotland from a Celtic to a feudal kingdom." How accurate is this statement?

5. How successfully did Henry II overcome the challenges that faced the monarchy when he became king?

### Historical Study: European and World

**EITHER**

**Nation and King**

6. To what extent was the Magna Carta a consequence of John's failure to retain Normandy?

7. "The growth in the power of the Capetian monarchy was entirely due to the abilities and leadership of Philip II." Discuss.

8. Was the victory at Stirling Bridge William Wallace's only important contribution to the Scottish struggle for independence?

9. How far was the Scottish victory in the Wars of Independence due to their own efforts rather than English failings?

**OR**

**Crisis of Authority**

10. To what extent was the Peasants' Revolt due to the Black Death?

11. What was the main cause of the Hundred Years' War?

12. How far was Scottish involvement the main cause of the English defeat in the Hundred Years' War?

13. "The move to Avignon was the most important reason for the decline of the power of the Papacy in the fourteenth and fifteenth centuries." Discuss.

## OPTION B: EARLY MODERN HISTORY

**Answer TWO questions, one from Historical Study: Scottish and British
and one from Historical Study: European and World**

### Historical Study: Scottish and British

**EITHER**

### Scotland in the Age of the Reformation 1542–1603

1. How great an influence did the "rough wooing", 1543–1548, have on Scottish politics?

2. To what extent did the Reformation of 1560 come about for political reasons?

3. How successful were the Regents in ruling Scotland between 1567 and 1580?

4. Was Andrew Melville the main cause of religious conflict during the reign of James VI up to 1603?

5. To what extent was the power of the Scottish Crown damaged between 1542 and 1603?

**OR**

### Scotland and England in the Century of Revolutions 1603–1702

6. How effective was James VI and I's rule in Scotland after the Union of Crowns, 1603?

7. "Eleven years of tyranny." How justified is this description of the personal rule of Charles I from 1629 to 1640?

8. "Parliament's actions between 1640 and 1642 were the most important cause of the outbreak of Civil War." How accurate is this statement?

9. How significant an impact did the Glorious Revolution of 1689 have on the government of Scotland and England?

10. To what extent did Parliament win in its struggles with the kings in the seventeenth century?

## Historical Study:  European and World

**EITHER**

### Royal Authority in 17th and 18th Century Europe

11. How important was Versailles to the power of the absolute monarchy of Louis XIV?

12. Did Louis XIV revoke the Edict of Nantes in 1685 for purely religious reasons?

13. How beneficial were Frederick II's social reforms in Prussia?

14. How successfully did Joseph II deal with religious issues in Austria?

**OR**

### The French Revolution:  The Emergence of the Citizen State

15. Which section of French society had the most cause for complaint under the Ancien Régime?

16. Why did the challenge to absolute monarchy develop into revolution in 1789?

17. To what extent was Robespierre responsible for the "Terror"?

18. How important was war in causing political instability in France in the 1790s?

**[Turn over**

## OPTION C:  LATER MODERN HISTORY

**Answer TWO questions, one from Historical Study:  Scottish and British
and one from Historical Study:  European and World**

### Historical Study:  Scottish and British

**Britain 1850s–1979**

1. "It was the militant suffragette campaign, more than any other factor, that led to the achievement of female suffrage in 1918."  How valid is this view?

2. How democratic had Britain become by 1928?

3. To what extent were the Liberal social reforms of 1906–1914 a response to the challenge from the Labour Party?

4. How successfully did the Labour government of 1945–1951 deal with the social problems identified in the Beveridge Report of 1942?

5. **Either**

   (a) Assess the impact of urbanisation on religion, education and leisure habits in Scotland between 1880 and 1939.

   **Or**

   (b) How far did attitudes in Scotland towards the Union change between 1880 and 1939?

**Historical Study: European and World**

**EITHER**

**The Growth of Nationalism**

6. To what extent was there a growth in nationalism in **either** Germany **or** Italy between 1815 and 1848?

7. **Either**

   (a) How important was Prussian economic growth in bringing about the unification of Germany by 1871?

   **Or**

   (b) "Foreign intervention was the main reason for the achievement of Italian unification by 1871." How justified is this view?

8. **Either**

   (a) How important was the leadership of Hitler in the rise of the Nazis to power in Germany by 1933?

   **Or**

   (b) How important was the leadership of Mussolini in the rise of the Fascists to power in Italy by 1922?

9. To what extent did Fascist governments rely on force to stay in power?

   Discuss with reference to **either** Nazi rule in Germany between 1933 and 1939 **or** Fascist rule in Italy between 1922 and 1939.

**OR**

**The Large Scale State**

*The USA*

10. To what extent were the difficulties faced by black Americans in the 1920s and 1930s due to the lack of action by the federal government?

11. "The Wall Street Crash was the principal reason for the depression of the 1930s." How justified is this view?

12. How important in restoring prosperity in the 1930s were the increased powers of the federal government under the New Deal?

13. "The Civil Rights campaign of the 1950s and 1960s concerned itself above all with the problems facing black Americans in the Southern states." How accurate is this statement?

*Russia*

14. "The power of the Church was the key factor in the stability of the Tsarist state in the years before 1905." How justified is this view?

15. How important was the work of Stolypin in the recovery of the Tsarist state after 1905?

16. To what extent was the Provisional Government responsible for its own downfall?

17. How effectively had the Bolsheviks established their authority over Russia by 1921?

*[END OF QUESTION PAPER]*

**[BLANK PAGE]**

# X044/302

| | | |
|---|---|---|
| NATIONAL<br>QUALIFICATIONS<br>2007 | FRIDAY, 18 MAY<br>10.40 AM – 12.05 PM | **HISTORY**<br>HIGHER<br>Paper 2 |

Answer questions on only **one** Special Topic.

Take particular care to show clearly the Special Topic chosen. On the **front** of the answer book, **in the top right-hand corner**, write the number of the Special Topic.

You are expected to use background knowledge appropriately in answering source-based questions.

Marks may be deducted for bad spelling and bad punctuation, and for writing that is difficult to read.

Some sources have been adapted or translated.

SCOTTISH
QUALIFICATIONS
AUTHORITY

[BLANK PAGE]

## OPTION A: MEDIEVAL HISTORY

## SPECIAL TOPIC 1: NORMAN CONQUEST AND EXPANSION 1050–1153

**Study the sources below and then answer the questions which follow.**

**Source A:** from William of Malmesbury, *Chronicles of the Kings of England,* written in the twelfth century.

Observing this, William gave a signal to his troops, that, pretending to flee, they should withdraw from the field. By this means, the solid formation of the English opened for the purpose of cutting down the fleeing enemy and thus brought upon itself swift destruction; for the Normans, facing about, attacked them, thus disordered, and compelled them to flee . . . But some of the English, getting possession of high ground, drove back the Normans, who in the heat of pursuit were struggling up the slope. By hurling their javelins and rolling down stones on them as they stood below, the English easily destroyed these Normans to a man. Besides, by a short passage with which the English were acquainted, they avoided a deep ditch and trod underfoot such a multitude of their enemies that the heaps of bodies made the hollow level with the plain. This alternating victory, first of one side and then of the other, continued so long as Harold lived to check the retreat; but when he fell, his brain pierced by an arrow, the flight of the English ceased not until night.

**Source B:** from *The Anglo-Saxon Chronicle, c* 1085.

If anyone would know what manner of man King William was, the glory that he obtained, and of how many lands he was lord, then will we describe him as we have known him, we who had looked upon him and who once lived at his court. This King William . . . was a very wise and great man, and more honoured and more powerful than any of his predecessors. He was mild to those good men who loved God, but severe beyond measure to those who stood against him. He founded a noble monastery [Battle Abbey] on the spot where God permitted him to conquer England and he established monks in it, and he made it very rich. In his days the great monastery at Canterbury was built, and many others also throughout England; moreover, this land was filled with monks who lived after the rule of St. Benedict; and such was the state of religion in his days that all who would, might observe the rules of their respective orders.

**Source C:** from Jim Bradbury, *The Battle of Hastings* (1998).

William punished the region with the most harsh of all his harsh measures in England, the harrying of the north. Harrying as a punishment was not new in England, but William's was so severe as to be long remembered . . . The conqueror sought out any rebel, and any who got in the way. His troops spread over a great distance, combing woodland and remote areas, leaving no hiding place unearthed. He wanted the whole region north of the Humber to be deprived of food. Houses and crops were destroyed, any living creature that crossed the path of William's troops was slaughtered till a great band of ashes and waste spread over Yorkshire . . . William's reign was hardly a happy one. At no time was he free from cares . . . within a decade he had obliterated the higher ranks of the Old English nobility. By the time of the Conqueror's death, the greater nobility in England was of continental descent.

**Source D:** a photograph of a Norman Motte and Bailey castle in Inverurie, known as the Bass.

**Source E:** from Fiona Watson, *Scotland: a History* (2001).

In Scotland, national legislation did exist, but kings of Scots knew better than to tamper with all the existing regional law. However, they did exert stricter control over much of Scotland through the formal establishment of sheriffdoms, most of which were in place by the mid-twelfth century. The sheriff was the key royal official at a local level, responsible for taxes necessary to maintain the royal household and national government and of course administering royal justice to the local population . . . However, the main legacy of David I was perhaps less his secular administration reforms . . . and more the fact that he actively encouraged the introduction to Scotland of a new . . . reformed monastic order. This marked a new phase in the economic, as well as spiritual, development of Western Europe.

*[END OF SOURCES FOR SPECIAL TOPIC 1]*

### SPECIAL TOPIC 1: NORMAN CONQUEST AND EXPANSION 1050–1153

**Answer *all* of the following questions.**

*Marks*

1. How fully does **Source A** explain the Norman victory at the Battle of Hastings?
   *Use the source and recalled knowledge.*    **6**

2. Compare the views in **Sources B** and **C** of William's dealings with his English subjects after the Battle of Hastings in 1066.
   *Compare the sources overall and in detail.*    **5**

3. How fully do **Sources A**, **B** and **C** show the success of the Norman conquest of England?
   *Use **Sources A**, **B** and **C** and recalled knowledge.*    **8**

4. How useful is **Source D** in demonstrating the Normanisation of Scotland by David I?
   *In reaching a conclusion you should refer to:*
   • *the origin and possible purpose of the source;*
   • *the content of the source;*
   • *recalled knowledge.*    **5**

5. How typical was the Scottish experience of the wider Norman achievement in Europe in the eleventh and twelfth centuries?
   *Use **Source E** and recalled knowledge.*    **6**

   **(30)**

*[END OF QUESTIONS ON SPECIAL TOPIC 1]*

## SPECIAL TOPIC 2: THE CRUSADES 1096–1204

**Study the sources below and then answer the questions which follow.**

**Source A:** from a letter written by Pope Gregory VII, written in 1074.

The person who brings this letter came to Rome to visit us on his recent return from Constantinople. He repeated what we had heard from many others, that a pagan race had overcome the Christians and with horrible cruelty had devastated everything almost to the walls of Constantinople, and were now governing the conquered lands . . . and that they had slain many thousands of Christians as if they were but sheep. If we love God and wish to be recognised as Christians, we should be filled with grief at the misfortune of this great empire and the murder of so many Christians. But simply to grieve is not our whole duty . . . Know, therefore, that we are trusting in the mercy of God and in the power of His might and that we are making preparations to send aid to the Christian empire . . . Therefore we beg you by the faith in which you are united through Christ . . . that you be moved to proper compassion by the wounds and blood of your brethren and the danger of the empire and that, for the sake of Christ, you undertake the difficult task of bringing aid to your brethren. Send messengers to us at once to inform us of what God may inspire you to do in this matter.

**Source B:** Peter the Hermit leads the People's Crusade, from a fourteenth century manuscript.

**Source C:** an account of the battle of Antioch, from the *Deeds of the Franks*, written *c*. 1100–1101.

Then six battle lines were formed from the forces within the city. In the first line, that is at the very head, was Hugh the Great with the Franks and the Count of Flanders; in the second, Duke Godfrey with his army; in the third was Robert the Norman with his knights; in the fourth, carrying with him the Lance of the Saviour, was the Bishop of Puy . . . The Turks, however, engaged them in battle and by shooting killed many of our men. They began to go forth from both sides and to surround our men on all sides, hurling, shooting and wounding them.

Then . . . there came out from the mountains, also, countless armies with white horses, whose standards were all white. And so, when our leaders saw this army, they were entirely ignorant as to what it was, and who they were, until they recognised the aid of Christ, among whose leaders was St. George . . . This is to be believed, for many of our men saw it . . . The Turks and the Persians in their turn cried out. Thereupon, we invoked the Living and True God and charged against them, and in the name of Jesus Christ and of the Holy Sepulchre we began the battle, and, God helping, we overcame them. But the terrified Turks took to flight.

**Source D:** from W. B. Bartlett, *God Wills It* (1999).

Weakened, as they no doubt were, it appears that they still made an impressive sight. Kerbogha, when he saw the army, somewhat belatedly asked for a truce. His approaches were ignored . . . Ignoring the Turkish firestorm the Franks pressed forward . . . The Turks fell back . . . and it is now that the weakness of the Muslim unity at this point in history was exposed. It was split by petty internal rivalries; it lacked unity and cohesion . . . Many Muslim leaders were inspired by the desire for personal gain rather than any sense of religious or political unity and many of them still seriously underestimated the threat posed by the Crusade . . . A significant number of Kerbogha's Emirs feared him. Some believed that if he were to defeat the Crusade, his power would become absolute. Fearful of their own position many decided to flee with their forces, leaving Kerbogha to his fate.

**Source E:** from Zoë Oldenbourg, *The Crusades* (1998).

Once again Richard negotiated and in the most courteous terms. What Richard offered Saladin was the setting up of the Kingdom of Jerusalem as a Muslim protectorate. Henry of Champagne as king would become a vassal of the Sultan and fight for him against his enemies. In Jerusalem, Christians should have possession of the Holy Sepulchre and free access to the Holy Places. Richard signed a treaty with Saladin. There was an exchange of civilities which says less about the spirit of mutual understanding between them than about their haste to put an end to fighting. For Richard, who was no diplomat, it was a matter of saving face . . . The duke of Burgundy and his French barons did not approve of this policy and were disgusted to find themselves unwilling accomplices in what they regarded as a shameful desertion.

*[END OF SOURCES FOR SPECIAL TOPIC 2]*

### SPECIAL TOPIC 2: THE CRUSADES 1096–1204

**Answer *all* of the following questions.**

*Marks*

1. How fully does **Source A** describe the Roman Church's motives in calling the First Crusade?
   *Use the source and recalled knowledge.*    **6**

2. How useful is **Source B** as evidence of the range of people who followed Peter the Hermit during the People's Crusade?
   *In reaching a conclusion you should refer to:*
   * *the origin and possible purpose of the source;*
   * *the content of the source;*
   * *recalled knowledge.*    **5**

3. Compare the reasons given in **Sources C** and **D** for the defeat of the Muslim army at the battle of Antioch.
   *Compare the sources overall and in detail.*    **5**

4. Why was the First Crusade such a success for the Crusaders?
   *Use **Sources A**, **C** and **D** and recalled knowledge.*    **8**

5. How accurately does **Source E** illustrate the decline of the crusading ideal by 1204?
   *Use the source and recalled knowledge.*    **6**

**(30)**

*[END OF QUESTIONS ON SPECIAL TOPIC 2]*

## OPTION B: EARLY MODERN HISTORY

## SPECIAL TOPIC 3: SCOTLAND 1689–1715

**Study the sources below and then answer the questions which follow.**

**Source A:** from Keith Brown, *Kingdom or Province? Scotland and the Regal Union* (1992).

The last year of William's reign was overshadowed by the additional problem of the death in 1701 of Princess Anne's last surviving child, the Duke of Gloucester. As Anne was William's only heir this left the succession vulnerable, especially when Louis XIV recognised Anne's Jacobite half brother. Consequently, the English Parliament passed the Act of Settlement, regulating the succession and making Sophia, the electress of Hanover, heir to Anne. Scottish intentions were ignored in making this decision, which was seen by the Scottish Parliament as another example of English arrogance. William's own unexpected death in March 1702 left the crown in the hands of an unhealthy, childless woman, and made a resolution of the succession urgent.

**Source B:** William Patterson's vision of a Scottish Colony, written in the 1690s.

The time and expense of navigation to China, Japan and the Spice Islands, and the East Indies, will be reduced by more than half, and the consumption of European commodities will soon be more than doubled. Trade will increase trade, and money will make money, and the trading world shall need no more work for their people, but rather need people for their work.

**Source C:** from Broun, Finlay & Lynch (eds), *Image and Identity* (1998).

By the end of the 1704 session the Hanoverian succession had still not been secured. Ideas of a federal union with England had been put forward as well as further reform of the Scottish constitution. Nevertheless, the English response to the drawn out Scottish problem was precise. Under the terms of the Aliens Act 1705, Scots would be treated as Aliens in England and Scottish exports would be banned from English markets . . . In addition, there were threats of an invading English military force into Scotland. Uncertainty about the succession, a possible Jacobite restoration to the Scottish throne and most importantly the strategic safety of England's northern border during the war of the Spanish Succession, ensured that a resolution of the instability of Scottish affairs had to be found.

**Source D:** from a speech made by Seton of Pitmedden, on the first Article of the Treaty, 2 November 1706.

In general, I may point out, that by this Union, we'll have access to all the advantages in commerce the English enjoy: we'll be able, with good government, to improve our national product, for the benefit of the whole island; and we'll have our Liberty, Property and Religion, secured under the protection of one Sovereign, and one Parliament of Great Britain . . .

Let us therefore, My Lord, after all these considerations approve this Article: and when the whole Treaty shall be duly examined and ratified, I am hopeful that this Parliament will return their most dutiful thanks to Her Majesty for her royal endeavours in promoting a lasting Union between both nations.

**Source E:** from a petition to the Duke of Queensberry, 1706.

There is a Treaty with England laid before your Grace and the honourable estates of parliament, which overturns the very constitution of this Ancient Kingdom, suppresses our monarchy, and extinguishes our Parliament. This Treaty subjects all our fundamental rights, overthrows our religion and liberty, destroys the government of our Church and surrenders all that is precious to us to the will of the English in a British Parliament . . . making this Ancient Kingdom of Scotland just another part of England . . .

We do therefore with all our right hearted countrymen, humbly ask your Grace that no union be hastily entered into with England . . . And that the Treaty agreed on between the Commissioners for Scotland and the Commissioners for England may be rejected.

*[END OF SOURCES FOR SPECIAL TOPIC 3]*

### SPECIAL TOPIC 3: SCOTLAND 1689–1715

**Answer *all* of the following questions.**

*Marks*

1. How important were the issues raised in **Source A** in causing poor relations between Scotland and England between 1701 and 1705?
   *Use the source and recalled knowledge.*                                                                6

2. How useful is **Source B** as evidence of the reasons for setting up the Darien scheme?
   *In reaching a conclusion you should refer to:*
   * *the origin and possible purpose of the source;*
   * *the content of the source;*
   * *recalled knowledge.*                                                                                   5

3. How fully does **Source C** explain why England wanted an incorporating Union?
   *Use the source and recalled knowledge.*                                                                6

4. Compare the attitudes towards Union revealed in **Sources D** and **E**.
   *Compare the sources overall and in detail.*                                                              5

5. How far do **Sources A**, **C** and **D** explain the reasons why the Scottish Parliament passed the Act of Union?
   *Use **Sources A, C** and **D** and recalled knowledge.*                                                  8

                                                                                                         (30)

*[END OF QUESTIONS ON SPECIAL TOPIC 3]*

## SPECIAL TOPIC 4: THE ATLANTIC SLAVE TRADE

**Study the sources below and then answer the questions which follow.**

**Source A:** from Eric Williams, *"Slavery, Industrialisation and Abolition"* in D. Northrup (ed), *The Atlantic Slave Trade* (2002).

Britain was accumulating great wealth from the triangular trade. The demand for manufactured goods from that trade inevitably increased production. This industrial expansion required finance. What man was better able to afford the ready capital than a West Indian sugar planter or a Liverpool slave trader?

In June, 1783, the Prime Minister, Lord North, complimented the Quaker opponents of the slave trade on their humanity, but regretted that its abolition was an impossibility, as the trade had become necessary to almost every nation in Europe. Slave traders and sugar planters rubbed their hands in glee. The West Indian colonies were still the darlings of the Empire, the most precious jewels in the British crown.

**Source B:** from Olaudah Equiano, *Narrative of his Life* (1789).

One day, two of my wearied countrymen who were chained together, preferring death to such a life of misery, somehow made through the nettings and jumped into the sea. Immediately another quite dejected fellow, who on account of his illness was allowed to be out of irons, also followed their example, and I believe many more would very soon have done the same if they had not been prevented by the ship's crew. Two of the wretches were drowned, but they got the other and afterwards flogged him unmercifully for thus attempting to prefer death to slavery. In this manner we continued to undergo more hardships than I can now relate, hardships which are inseparable from this accursed trade.

**Source C:** from Earl Leslie Griggs, *Thomas Clarkson* (1936).

The value of Clarkson's services to the abolition of the slave trade is inestimable. Almost single-handed, he obtained the necessary witnesses for the various parliamentary investigations of the slave trade. He provided Wilberforce with the convincing evidence which made Wilberforce's speeches so graphic and appealing. He had spread propaganda from one end of the country to the other. No task was too great, no labour too small. Let it be remembered that Clarkson, the first great propagandist, was more instrumental than anyone else in discovering and presenting to the English people the true picture of the slave trade.

**Source D:** from a letter to Wilberforce by Samuel Hoare, February 1792.

The members of the Church of England have put forward an idea that the Dissenters wish for a revolution, and that the abolition of the slave trade is somewhat connected with it. I hope this has no foundation. However, some enquiries of Mr Clarkson have added to this belief. In some letters he declares that he is a friend to the French Revolution. If I knew where he was, I would write to him on the subject.

A moment's reflection must convince him that there is too much reason to fear that his own private thoughts will be considered an opinion of our committee. I hope you will lose no time in giving him a hint upon this subject, or our cause will be severely injured.

**Source E:** from Hugh Thomas, *The Slave Trade* (1997).

But there was opposition. Bamber Gascoyne even said that he was "persuaded that the slave trade might be made a much greater source of revenue and riches . . . than it was at present".

His fellow Member for Liverpool, Lord Penrhyn, said that, were the Commons to vote for abolition, "they actually would strike at seventy million pounds worth of property, they would ruin the colonies, and by destroying an essential nursery of seamen, give up British control of the sea at a single stroke".

The members of Parliament for London also strongly opposed abolition. Alderman Sawbridge opposed Wilberforce on the ground that abolition would not serve Africans. "If they could not be sold as slaves, they would be butchered and executed at home."

*[END OF SOURCES FOR SPECIAL TOPIC 4]*

### SPECIAL TOPIC 4: THE ATLANTIC SLAVE TRADE

**Answer *all* of the following questions.**

*Marks*

1. How accurately does **Source A** reflect the attitude of British governments to the slave trade in the eighteenth century?
   *Use the source and recalled knowledge.*                                                           **6**

2. How useful is **Source B** as evidence of the slave experience on board ship?
   *In reaching a conclusion you should refer to:*
   - *the origin and possible purpose of the source;*
   - *the content of the source;*
   - *recalled knowledge.*                                                                              **5**

3. How fully does **Source C** identify the methods used by the abolitionists to promote their cause?
   *Use the source and recalled knowledge.*                                                            **6**

4. To what extent does the evidence in **Source D** support **Source C**'s assessment of Clarkson's contribution to the abolition of the slave trade?
   *Compare the sources overall and in detail.*                                                        **5**

5. How fully do **Sources A**, **D** and **E** illustrate the difficulties faced by the abolitionists in their campaign?
   *Use **Sources A**, **D** and **E** and recalled knowledge.*                                        **8**

                                                                                                   **(30)**

*[END OF QUESTIONS ON SPECIAL TOPIC 4]*

## SPECIAL TOPIC 5: THE AMERICAN REVOLUTION

**Study the sources below and then answer the questions which follow.**

**Source A:** from a letter sent by John Dickinson, a farmer from Pennsylvania, to the inhabitants of the British colonies, May 1774.

Great Britain follows a policy of suppressing the freedom of America by a military force, to be supported by money taken out of our pockets . . . The people in Britain are misled into a belief that we are in a state of rebellion . . . The minister addressing the House of Commons calls the stoppage of the port of Boston "a punishment inflicted on those who have disobeyed Parliament". Surely you cannot doubt at this time, my countrymen, but that the people of Massachusetts Bay are suffering in a cause common to us all.

I offer some observations concerning the measures that may be most effective in the present emergency. Other nations have fought for their liberty, and have judged the prize worth the price that was paid for it. These colonies need not go as far as that. So dependent is Great Britain on us for supplies, that heaven seems to have placed in our hands the means of an effective, yet peaceable resistance. A general agreement between these colonies on non-importation and non-exportation faithfully observed would certainly be successful.

**Source B:** from Peter D. G. Thomas, *Revolution in America* (1992).

Of immediate significance was the misunderstanding by Congress of British opinion, and the American belief in the effectiveness of a refusal to trade with Britain. Although Congress had rejected military action, it had nevertheless deliberately challenged Britain. Congress was bluffing, confident that Britain would again give ground, as in 1766 and 1770. This time Britain did not do so, and called the colonial bluff. The delegates at the Second Continental Congress in May 1775 faced an armed conflict which most of them did not want. Hostilities had accidentally already commenced. The war of independence was the result of a political miscalculation by a Congress that had chosen to avoid a military conflict and yet blundered into one.

**Source C:** from David F. Burg, *The American Revolution* (2001).

The Continental Congress met at the State House in Philadelphia, where delegates began to consider the issue of American independence from Great Britain. Already in early January (1776) New Hampshire became the first of the colonies to establish an independent government, whereas the Maryland Convention . . . followed the stance that avoided any support of independence for the colonies. At the same time, however, the drive towards independence received a huge boost with the publication in Philadelphia of Thomas Paine's *Common Sense*, which argued that efforts at reconciliation were useless and strongly urged creation of an independent, continental republic . . . Widely distributed and read, *Common Sense* favourably impressed and persuaded not only such leaders as Adams and Washington, but also tens of thousands of their fellow Americans.

**Source D:** from a diary entry by Christopher Marshall, 17 January 1778, Valley Forge.

My mind seems anxiously concerned on account of our distressed friends and acquaintances with our brave General Washington, as he and his army are now obliged to encounter all the severity of this cold weather, as they with him are living out in the woods with little shelter. Our poor friends in town [Philadelphia] have need of fuel and other necessaries, while the British supporters, under the protection of that savage monster Howe, are revelling in luxury and drunkenness, without any feelings for the distress of their (once happy) bleeding country.

**Source E:** from the *New York Journal*, 18 May 1778.

At last we have news from France that Congress has concluded a treaty of alliance with the King of the French. His Most Christian Majesty guarantees the independence, sovereignty, liberties, and all the possessions of the United States of America; and Congress, on its part, guarantees all the dominions of the French king in the West Indies. No monopoly of our trade is desired. It is left open to us whom we choose to trade with. We are, moreover, to be assisted generously with all kinds of supplies . . . The Treaties were signed on the sixth of February.

*[END OF SOURCES FOR SPECIAL TOPIC 5]*

### SPECIAL TOPIC 5: THE AMERICAN REVOLUTION

**Answer *all* of the following questions.**

*Marks*

1. How fully does **Source A** identify the reasons for the colonial challenge to British control of America by 1774?
   *Use the source and recalled knowledge.*                                                                    **7**

2. Compare the views expressed in **Sources A** and **B** on colonial actions after the passing of the Coercive Acts in 1774.
   *Compare the sources overall and in detail.*                                                                **5**

3. How fully do **Sources A**, **B**, and **C** illustrate the issues that led the Americans to declare independence from Britain in 1776?
   *Use **Sources A**, **B** and **C** and recalled knowledge.*                                                **8**

4. How valuable is **Source D** to an understanding of Washington's difficulties in fighting the war against Britain?
   *In reaching a conclusion you should refer to:*
   - *the origin and possible purpose of the source;*
   - *the content of the source;*
   - *recalled knowledge.*                                                                                     **5**

5. How important was foreign intervention in the outcome of the war?
   *Use **Source E** and recalled knowledge.*                                                                  **5**

                                                                                                              **(30)**

*[END OF QUESTIONS ON SPECIAL TOPIC 5]*

## OPTION C: LATER MODERN HISTORY

### SPECIAL TOPIC 6: PATTERNS OF MIGRATION: SCOTLAND 1830s–1930s

**Study the sources below and then answer the questions which follow.**

**Source A:** from Danny McGowan, "Scotland, Sectarianism, and the Irish diaspora", in *Frontline Online*, the website of the International Socialist Movement, Issue 4, 22 October 2001.

Immigrants meet racism rather than create it. Large-scale immigration did not cause anti-Irish racism, but it gave a focus for existing hostility. General contempt for the poor was reinforced by racial stereotypes. The Irish migrated to an urban squalor where drink offered a temporary escape, yet found themselves blamed for causing the squalor through their own drunkenness. Their communities were criminalised and subject to excessive police surveillance. Though the idea of an Irish "threat" still figures in some historical explanations, they were "despised rather than actively feared".

**Source B:** from the *Ayr Advertiser*, 1849.

The influence of the Irish on older people, though quite considerable, must be small when compared with their influence on the young population. Mixing as they must with Irish of their own age, they will, at the most easily influenced time of their lives, receive impressions from their vicious Irish companions. In future years this will not either promote the private welfare of young Scots or that of Scotland. While we earnestly hope for the recovery of Ireland from her degraded position so that this plague of immigrants in time may be halted, we are called upon to another task – that of meeting the evil as it already exists by the weapons of religion and education.

**Source C:** from a letter sent by Godfrey McKinnon in Australia to John McDonald in Uist, 1864.

I had very hard work of it the first three years that I was in this country but now I can take it a little easier. I have done very well for all the time I have been here, more than if I had been in Skye for the rest of my life, even if I were to live for fifty years or more. I have got a beautiful piece of country and first rate stock of sheep, cattle and horses. I have gone to great expense with my sheep purchases – imported rams. It will pay me very well in a few years. I had a splendid clip of wool this season and I expect an even better clip next season.

**Source D:** from a report by the Immigration Agent for Victoria, Australia, 1853.

I do not consider that the inhabitants of the Islands of Scotland are well suited to the wants and needs of this colony. Their total ignorance of the English language makes it difficult to get employment for them, while their laziness and extremely filthy habits have not made a good impression on the British people already here. It would be better if such immigration was restricted at least, since these wretches have little of worth to offer this society. Indeed, it cannot be argued other than that their arrival is having a most unwelcome and detrimental effect on the inhabitants of this colony.

**Source E:** from Jenni Calder, *Scots in Canada* (2004).

The individual experiences of emigrant Scots varied, but even those who felt most positively about their new lives in Canada did not necessarily want to lose their Scottishness, nor did it seem becoming Canadian required that. Shinty came to Canada with the Scots, and out of it was born ice hockey. Indeed, as the many Scottish societies suggest, the more integrated these migrants became, the more important it became not just to preserve a Scottish identity but to maintain links with other Scots.

An important part of the role of Scottish societies in Canada was to look after their own, in a way that might not have seemed appropriate or necessary in the old country. Many Highland societies, as well as promoting Highland music and dancing, became the focus of Highland sporting activities. A piece in the *Celtic Monthly* of July 1893 states that "the national sentiment is stimulated because of the manly exercises of the Highland games of the old home being kept alive". These events were mainly for those who identified themselves as being of Scottish origin, but they were also spectacles that could hardly fail to have an impact on whatever community hosted them.

*[END OF SOURCES FOR SPECIAL TOPIC 6]*

### SPECIAL TOPIC 6: PATTERNS OF MIGRATION: SCOTLAND 1830s–1930s

*Marks*

**Answer *all* of the following questions.**

1. How accurate is the explanation in **Source A** for anti-Irish attitudes in nineteenth-century Scotland?
   *Use the source and recalled knowledge.*                                                                                                    **6**

2. To what extent does the evidence in **Source B** support the views expressed in **Source A**?
   *Compare the sources overall and in detail.*                                                                                                **5**

3. How useful is **Source C** as evidence of the success of Scottish emigrants in their new lands?
   *In reaching a conclusion you should refer to:*
   * *the origin and possible purpose of the source;*
   * *the content of the source;*
   * *recalled knowledge.*                                                                                                                     **5**

4. How typical are the views expressed in **Source D** of the attitudes towards Scots in the lands to which they emigrated in the nineteenth century?
   *Use the source and recalled knowledge.*                                                                                                    **6**

5. How fully do **Sources C**, **D** and **E** illustrate the experiences of Scots emigrants between the 1830s and 1930s?
   *Use **Sources C**, **D** and **E** and recalled knowledge.*                                                                                **8**

                                                                                                                                              **(30)**

*[END OF QUESTIONS ON SPECIAL TOPIC 6]*

## SPECIAL TOPIC 7: APPEASEMENT AND THE ROAD TO WAR, TO 1939

**Study the sources below and then answer the questions which follow.**

**Source A:** from Ian Kershaw, *Making Friends with Hitler: Lord Londonderry and Britain's Road to War* (2004).

The German ambassador in London read out to Eden the German memorandum justifying the remilitarisation of the Rhineland and blaming the Franco-Soviet treaty for the violation of Locarno. It also put forward Hitler's skilfully devised offer – certain to calm public opinion in Britain – to reach new agreements. These would involve non aggression pacts for a duration of 25 years with his neighbours, a new demilitarised zone now on both sides of the border, a western air force agreement and German re-entry to the League of Nations.

Prime Minister Baldwin's government was only too aware that public opinion was opposed to any risk of war and was largely supportive of Germany. It was even more aware of British military weakness. So it left the French in no doubt that Britain was unwilling to take any steps that would risk military involvement with Germany.

**Source B:** from a letter by Douglas Reed, foreign correspondent of *The Times*, to his editor, March 1938.

I believe it is already too late. Britain's military defeat is coming. I saw the German fighting machine enter Austria. It is terrifying. Indeed worse than anything I imagined, and you will realise that is saying a great deal . . . In my wildest nightmares I had not imagined anything so perfectly organised . . . The vital thing to remember is they want to destroy Britain.

In May 1936, I wrote some articles about these coming dangers which you did not use at the time because you thought they were too alarmist.

**Source C:** a cartoon by David Low, published in the *Evening Standard*, 10 September 1938. The figure in the soldier's pocket represents Henlein, the Sudeten Nazi leader. The figure holding the lamb represents Benes, the leader of Czechoslovakia.

## "HE ONLY WANTS TO LIE DOWN WITH YOUR LAMB"

**Source D:** from a speech by Neville Chamberlain in the House of Commons, 3 October 1938.

I think it is very essential not to forget certain things when the terms of the Munich agreement are being considered. All the elements were present for the outbreak of a conflict which might have brought about the catastrophe. In the Sudetenland, we had extremists on both sides ready to work up and provoke incidents. We had considerable quantities of arms which were not confined to regular armies. Therefore, it was essential that we should quickly reach a conclusion, so that this painful and difficult operation of transfer might be carried out at the earliest possible moment.

Before giving a verdict upon the Munich agreement, we should do well to avoid describing it as a personal or a national triumph for anyone. The real triumph is that it has shown that representatives of four great powers can find it possible to agree on a way of carrying out a difficult and delicate operation by discussion instead of by force of arms. Thereby, they have averted a catastrophe which would have ended civilisation as we have known it. The relief at our escape from this great peril of war has, I think, everywhere been mingled in this country with a profound feeling of sympathy.

I have nothing to be ashamed of.

**Source E:** from a speech by the Labour leader, Clement Attlee, in the House of Commons, 3 October 1938.

We all feel relief that war has not come this time. Every one of us has been passing through days of anxiety. We cannot, however, feel that peace has been established, but that we have nothing but an armistice in a state of war. We have been unable to go in for carefree rejoicing. We have felt that we are in the midst of a tragedy. We have felt humiliation. This has not been a victory for reason and humanity. It has been a victory for brute force. At every stage of the proceedings, there have been time limits laid down by the owner and ruler of armed force. The terms have not been negotiated; they have been terms laid down as ultimata. We have seen today a gallant, civilised and democratic people betrayed and handed over to a ruthless dictatorship. We have seen something more. We have seen the cause of democracy, which is, in our view, the cause of civilisation and humanity, receive a terrible defeat.

*[END OF SOURCES FOR SPECIAL TOPIC 7]*

### SPECIAL TOPIC 7: APPEASEMENT AND THE ROAD TO WAR, TO 1939

**Answer *all* of the following questions.**

*Marks*

1. To what extent does **Source A** explain why Britain did not take strong action against Germany immediately after the remilitarisation of the Rhineland?
   *Use the source and recalled knowledge.*                                                              6

2. How fully does **Source B** illustrate British opinion towards the Anschluss?
   *Use the source and recalled knowledge.*                                                              6

3. How valuable is **Source C** as evidence of British attitudes towards the crisis over Czechoslovakia in 1938?
   *In reaching a conclusion you should refer to:*
   - *the origin and possible purpose of the source;*
   - *the content of the source;*
   - *recalled knowledge.*                                                                               5

4. Compare the views expressed in **Sources D** and **E** on the Munich agreement.
   *Compare the sources overall and in detail.*                                                          5

5. To what extent was the British policy of appeasement justified in view of the issues facing Britain in the 1930s?
   *Use **Sources B, C** and **D** and recalled knowledge.*                                              8

*[END OF QUESTIONS ON SPECIAL TOPIC 7]*

**(30)**

**SPECIAL TOPIC 8: THE ORIGINS AND DEVELOPMENT OF THE COLD WAR 1945–1985**

**Study the sources below and then answer the questions which follow.**

**Source A:** from the Resolution of the Council of Ministers of the German Democratic Republic, 12 August 1961.

The desire for revenge has intensified in West Germany, with increasing territorial claims against the German Democratic Republic and neighbouring states. This is closely tied to accelerated rearmament and the acquisition of nuclear weapons by West Germany. The Adenauer administration is making preparations for civil war against the GDR. West German and West Berlin espionage headquarters are systematically putting citizens of the GDR under pressure and organising the smuggling of human beings.

For all these reasons, the Council of Ministers of the GDR is taking the following measures to secure peace in Europe and protect the GDR . . . A border control will be introduced at the borders to the GDR, including the borders with West Berlin. Borders to West Berlin will be sufficiently guarded and effectively controlled to prevent subversive activities from the West.

**Source B:** from an address by the Vice-President of the United States, Lyndon B. Johnson, to the Berlin Parliament, 19 August 1961.

This crisis has arisen because of a massive fact of history. The free men of Germany – both here and in West Germany – have succeeded since the end of the war beyond our most optimistic hopes. I am not referring only to their economic success, which all the world knows and admires. They succeeded in far more important ways. They have built a vital democratic life . . . They have played a great constructive role in making a united Europe. They are now coming to play a major role on the world scene.

Meanwhile, in East Germany, there has been a terrible and tragic failure. Despite the use of force and propaganda, the Communists have not been able to create a life to which men can commit their talents, their faith, and the future of their children.

Make no mistake. This fact of history is well understood in the Kremlin. What they are trying to do now is to place barbed wire, bayonets, and tanks against the forces of history.

**Source C:** from J. Young and J. Kent, *International Relations since 1945* (2004).

The risks that were run during the Cuban Missile Crisis, and indeed the reasons for running them, have probably been overstated. At the end of the day neither leader was likely to have ordered a major nuclear strike for the sake of strategic benefits that were more apparent than real. Yet there were serious risks . . .

There was the danger of local commanders seizing the initiative and dragging their superiors into a conflict they would have wanted at all costs to avoid. Not only did the US Navy clash with the Soviets, but a local commander in Cuba, acting on his own authority, shot down an American U2 spy plane on 25th October. In addition, General Tommy Power, the head of the US Strategic Air Command, placed his forces on DEFCON 2 (Defence Condition 2) and prepared for immediate action without consulting the White House.

The flaws in the decision-making process and the chain of command could have led to a nuclear clash because of the level of brinkmanship, despite the politicians' desire to avoid any such conflict.

**Source D:** from the Action Programme of the Communist Party of Czechoslovakia, 5 April 1968.

Comrades

We are not changing our basic beliefs.  We want to develop to the utmost in this country an advanced socialist society, which will be economically, technologically, and socially highly advanced.  It will be socially and nationally just, and democratically organised.

We want to start building up a new, strongly democratic model of a socialist society which will fully correspond to Czechoslovak conditions.

Our own experiences and Marxist knowledge lead us jointly to the conclusion that these aims cannot be achieved along the old paths . . .

We want to set new forces of socialist life in motion, to make possible a much more effective social system and to demonstrate fully the advantages of socialism.

**Source E:** from E. J Hobsbawm, *The Age of Extremes* (1995).

The Action Programme of the Czechoslovak Communist Party might or might not have been – just – acceptable to the Soviet Union.  However, the cohesion, perhaps the very existence, of the East European Soviet bloc seemed to be at stake, as the "Prague Spring" revealed and increased the cracks within it.  Hard-line regimes without mass support, such as Poland and East Germany, feared internal destabilisation from the Czech example, which they criticised bitterly.  As a result, the Russians decided to overthrow the Prague regime by military force.

This held the Soviet bloc together for another twenty years, but henceforth only by the threat of Soviet military intervention.  In the last twenty years of the Soviet bloc, even the leadership of the ruling communist parties appeared to have lost any real belief in what they were doing.

*[END OF SOURCES FOR SPECIAL TOPIC 8]*

### SPECIAL TOPIC 8: THE ORIGINS AND DEVELOPMENT OF THE COLD WAR 1945–1985

**Answer *all* of the following questions.**

*Marks*

1. How useful is **Source A** as evidence of East Germany's attitude towards West Berlin in 1961?
   *In reaching a conclusion you should refer to:*
   - *the origin and possible purpose of the source;*
   - *the content of the source;*
   - *recalled knowledge.*                                                                          **5**

2. Compare the attitudes towards the Berlin Crisis of 1961 expressed in **Sources A** and **B**.
   *Compare the sources overall and in detail.*                                                     **5**

3. How accurate is the assessment in **Source C** of the risks of conflict during the Cuban Missile Crisis of 1962?
   *Use the source and recalled knowledge.*                                                         **6**

4. To what extent does **Source D** explain the aims of the reform movement in Czechoslovakia in 1968?
   *Use the source and recalled knowledge.*                                                         **6**

5. How fully did differences in ideology explain the reasons for tension between the Superpowers during the Cold War?
   *Use **Sources A**, **C** and **E** and recalled knowledge.*                                      **8**

*[END OF QUESTIONS ON SPECIAL TOPIC 8]*

**(30)**

## SPECIAL TOPIC 9: IRELAND 1900–1985: A DIVIDED IDENTITY

**Study the sources below and then answer the questions which follow.**

**Source A:** from a speech by the Irish Nationalist MP, John Dillon, in the House of Commons, 15 April 1912.

We look forward to this Home Rule Bill with hope and enthusiasm. The Ireland we look forward to under this Bill is an Ireland which will become self-supporting and will be ready to take its share in all the burdens of the British Empire. Ireland will do so, not as an unwilling slave, but as a willing partner. We will take a willing share, not only by contributing to the financial burdens of the Empire, but we shall contribute what is greater than that, namely the bravery of our sons.

I tell the men of Ulster, and the Protestants of Ireland, that, if they will only join us in the great effort to realise this dream, they will find that the day on which they make up their minds to trust their own countrymen will be the happiest day in the history of Ireland.

**Source B:** from a speech by the Ulster Unionist MP, William Moore, in the House of Commons, 15 April 1912.

I want to say what my policy is. I say solemnly here that, as long as they have a drop of blood in their veins, Ulster men will do their best to make the government in Ulster by the Nationalist Party impossible. We shall leave no stone unturned, but do our best to make every effort to carry out that policy successfully. We pledged our lives to this policy the other day in Belfast.

If you are going to plant Home Rule, you cannot do it until you have wiped us out, and the blood will be on your hands, and not on ours.

If, without my consent, you transfer my allegiance to a new Constitution proposed without my consent; if you propose to sell me into a political slavery under the new Constitution you are setting up, I say that I do not regard it as rebelling to resist that to the best of my ability and, please God, I shall do it.

**Source C:** from F. S. L. Lyons, *Ireland since the Famine* (1973).

All the passion and determination which Sinn Féin had been able to mobilise against the threat of military service was thrown behind it in the general election of 1918. It did not matter that many Sinn Féin candidates were in prison, or that their manifesto was heavily censored. On the contrary, these government actions were an advantage.

Sinn Féin's message was a restatement of the republican ideal, which was to be achieved by a four-point policy. First, they would withdraw from Westminster: second, to make use of any means available to weaken the power of Britain to control Ireland by military force: third, the establishment of a constituent assembly as the supreme authority for Ireland: finally, to appeal to the Peace Conference at Versailles to establish Ireland as an independent nation. Such a programme proved irresistible.

**Source D:** from a speech by Count George N. Plunkett in the Dail Eireann during a debate on the Anglo-Irish Treaty, 19 December 1921.

We should reject this Treaty because it goes against the conscience of the Irish people.

We are told that our national liberties will be secured by handing them over to the authority of the British Government. British rule was rejected, not only by our generation, but by past generations of fighting men. We are now told that we must swear an oath of allegiance to the English king, and that this is the only means by which we will achieve our liberty.

I am not going to abandon the cause to which I have devoted my life. I am no more an enemy of peace than Arthur Griffith, but I will never sacrifice the independence of Ireland simply to stop the fighting. We have taken an oath of loyalty to the Republic. Are we going to take a false oath now to King George?

**Source E:** from M. Hopkinson, *Green against Green: The Irish Civil War* (1988).

The Irish Civil War revealed the gap between political reality and political desires among Irish nationalists. It was fought over the way in which the Anglo-Irish Treaty defined the new Irish state's relationship to Britain.

To the Republicans, the Treaty betrayed the commitment to an Irish republic, completely independent of Britain, leaving Ireland in effect a British dominion, although with significant powers of self-government.

To the pro-Treaty side, it was the best offer available in the circumstances. In the words of Michael Collins, it gave Ireland "freedom – not the ultimate freedom that all nations desire and develop to, but the freedom to achieve it."

Strangely, the partition of Ireland was hardly an issue at all in the war.

*[END OF SOURCES FOR SPECIAL TOPIC 9]*

**SPECIAL TOPIC 9: IRELAND 1900–1985: A DIVIDED IDENTITY**

**Answer *all* of the following questions.**

*Marks*

1. How useful is **Source A** as evidence of Irish attitudes towards the policy of Home Rule at the time?
   *In reaching a conclusion you should refer to:*
   * *the origin and possible purpose of the source;*
   * *the content of the source;*
   * *recalled knowledge.*                                                                                         5

2. Compare the views on the Home Rule Bill of 1912 expressed in **Sources A** and **B**.
   *Compare the sources overall and in detail.*                                                                   5

3. How fully does **Source C** explain the reasons for the growth in support for Sinn Féin in the election of 1918?
   *Use the source and recalled knowledge.*                                                                        6

4. To what extent did the views expressed in **Source D** reflect Irish opinion towards the Peace Treaty with Britain?
   *Use the source and recalled knowledge.*                                                                        6

5. To what extent do **Sources B**, **C** and **E** illustrate the difficulties in achieving peace in Ireland between 1912 and 1922?
   *Use **Sources B**, **C** and **E** and recalled knowledge.*                                                    8

                                                                                                                 **(30)**

*[END OF QUESTIONS ON SPECIAL TOPIC 9]*

*[END OF QUESTION PAPER]*

[BLANK PAGE]

[BLANK PAGE]

# X044/301

NATIONAL
QUALIFICATIONS
2008

MONDAY, 26 MAY
9.00 AM – 10.20 AM

# HISTORY
# HIGHER
Paper 1

Answer questions on **one** Option only.

Take particular care to show clearly the Option chosen. On the **front** of the answer book, **in the top right-hand corner**, write A or B or C.

Within the Option chosen, answer **two** questions, one from Historical Study: Scottish and British and one from Historical Study: European and World.

All questions are assigned 20 marks.

Marks may be deducted for bad spelling and bad punctuation, and for writing that is difficult to read.

[BLANK PAGE]

## OPTION A:  MEDIEVAL HISTORY

**Answer TWO questions, one from Historical Study:  Scottish and British
and one from Historical Study:  European and World**

### Historical Study:  Scottish and British

**Medieval Society**

1. "In 12th Century Scotland and England, the strengths of the Feudal System considerably outweighed its weaknesses."  How accurate is this view?

2. How great an impact did the regular Church have on Medieval Society?

3. To what extent can it be argued that events such as the Investiture Contest indicate that the medieval Church was more interested in politics than religion?

4. How important was the development of the Scottish economy in strengthening the powers of the Crown during the reign of David I?

5. To what extent was the dispute between Henry II and Becket a continuation of the wider struggle between Church and State?

### Historical Study:  European and World

**EITHER**

**Nation and King**

6. "History has judged him to be a failure."  How valid is this view of the reign of King John (1199–1216)?

7. How important was the weakness of baronial opposition in the strengthening of the power of the French monarchy during the reign of Philip Augustus?

8. How successful was Louis IX in expanding the power of the French monarchy?

9. To what extent was Robert Bruce more concerned with personal ambition than with Scottish independence?

**OR**

**Crisis of Authority**

10. To what extent was the eventual French victory in the Hundred Years' War due to the contribution of Joan of Arc?

11. How important were uprisings such as the Jacquerie and the Peasants' Revolt in causing the decline of serfdom?

12. "The impact of the Black Death upon medieval society was not entirely harmful."  How valid is this view?

13. To what extent did the Great Schism reduce the authority of the Church?

## OPTION B: EARLY MODERN HISTORY

**Answer TWO questions, one from Historical Study: Scottish and British and one from Historical Study: European and World**

### Historical Study: Scottish and British

**EITHER**

**Scotland in the Age of the Reformation 1542–1603**

1. How successful was the Roman Catholic Church in its attempts to reform itself before 1560?

2. How far was the death of Mary of Guise the main reason for the success of the Protestant Reformation in Scotland?

3. To what extent was Mary Queen of Scots herself to blame for the loss of her throne in 1567?

4. "Mary's forced abdication was the main reason for political instability in Scotland in the period 1567–1585." How valid is this view?

5. How significant were James VI's relations with the Church in his attempts to strengthen royal authority up to 1603?

**OR**

**Scotland and England in the Century of Revolutions 1603–1702**

6. How far were religious issues the main threat to royal authority under James VI and I?

7. How important were Charles I's financial policies in weakening his authority in the years before the Civil War?

8. "Purely a response to the attempts of Charles I to impose his religious views on Scotland." How valid is this view of the growth of the Covenanting movement?

9. To what extent was the Republic successful in overcoming its problems between 1649 and 1660?

10. How successful was the Glorious Revolution in limiting the powers of the Crown?

## Historical Study:  European and World

**EITHER**

**Royal Authority in 17th and 18th Century Europe**

11. How successfully did Louis XIV increase the power of the monarchy during his reign?

12. To what extent should the credit for Louis XIV's achievements be given to his ministers?

13. How far did the enlightened reforms of Frederick II lead to significant changes to life in Prussia?

14. To what extent was Joseph II himself responsible for the limited success of his reforms?

**OR**

**The French Revolution:  The Emergence of the Citizen State**

15. How far were the ideas of the Enlightenment the most serious challenge to the Ancien Regime?

16. To what extent was the decision to abolish the monarchy in 1792 a result of the pressures of war?

17. How effective was the government of the Jacobin dictatorship, 1793–1794?

18. To what extent had the Ancien Regime been destroyed by 1799?

**[Turn over**

## OPTION C: LATER MODERN HISTORY

**Answer TWO questions, one from Historical Study: Scottish and British
and one from Historical Study: European and World**

*Page six*

### Historical Study: Scottish and British

**Britain 1850s–1979**

1. To what extent was the growth of democracy in Britain after 1860 due to social and economic change?

2. How important were concerns about the extent of poverty in Britain in the Liberal Government's decision to introduce social reforms between 1906 and 1914?

3. "Their contribution during World War I was the main reason why the majority of women gained the right to vote in 1918." How valid is this view?

4. How successful was the National Government in dealing with the difficulties caused by the Depression of the 1930s?

5. **Either**

   (a) To what extent did urbanisation increase social divisions in Scotland, 1880–1939? Discuss with reference to religion, leisure and education.

   **Or**

   (b) "Political nationalism in Scotland only became a serious force from the 1960s onwards." How accurate is this view?

## Historical Study:  European and World

**EITHER**

**The Growth of Nationalism**

*Germany*

6. How important was Bismarck's leadership in the achievement of German unification?

7. How successful was the new German state in winning popular support during the period 1871–1914?

8. How important were weaknesses and divisions among his opponents in explaining Hitler's rise to power by 1933?

9. To what extent did the Nazis' control of Germany up to 1939 depend on their social and economic policies?


*Italy*

10. How significant was the military leadership of Garibaldi in the achievement of Italian unification?

11. How successful was the new Italian state in winning popular support during the period 1871–1914?

12. How important were weaknesses and divisions among his opponents in explaining Mussolini's rise to power by 1922?

13. To what extent did the Fascists' control of Italy up to 1939 depend on their social and economic policies?


**[Turn over for The Large Scale State on *Page eight***

OR

**The Large Scale State**

*The USA*

14. "Economically, socially, and politically divided." How accurate is this view of American society in the 1920s?

15. To what extent was the growth of the Ku Klux Klan in the 1920s a result of increasing concerns over immigration?

16. To what extent was the Depression of the 1930s the result of the economic boom of the 1920s?

17. How far were improvements in the lives of black Americans by 1968 due to the Civil Rights movement?

*Russia*

18. "In the period before 1905, opposition groups had little chance of mounting an effective challenge to the authority of the Tsarist state." How accurate is this statement?

19. To what extent was the outbreak of revolution in 1905 due to Russia's social and economic problems?

20. How important was Russia's military failure in the First World War in causing the collapse of Tsarist authority in 1917?

21. To what extent was the establishment and survival of the Soviet state between 1917 and 1921 due to the weaknesses and divisions of the Bolsheviks' opponents?

*[END OF QUESTION PAPER]*

# X044/302

| | | |
|---|---|---|
| NATIONAL<br>QUALIFICATIONS<br>2008 | MONDAY, 26 MAY<br>10.40 AM – 12.05 PM | **HISTORY**<br>HIGHER<br>Paper 2 |

Answer questions on only **one** Special Topic.

Take particular care to show clearly the Special Topic chosen. On the **front** of the answer book, **in the top right-hand corner**, write the number of the Special Topic.

You are expected to use background knowledge appropriately in answering source-based questions.

Marks may be deducted for bad spelling and bad punctuation, and for writing that is difficult to read.

Some sources have been adapted or translated.

[BLANK PAGE]

## OPTION A: MEDIEVAL HISTORY

### SPECIAL TOPIC 1: NORMAN CONQUEST AND EXPANSION 1050–1153

**Study the sources below and then answer the questions which follow.**

**Source A:** Duke William's message to Harold before the Battle of Hastings, from *The Deeds of William, Duke of the Normans and King of the English,* written *c.* 1071 by William of Poitiers.

Archbishop Stigand and Earl Godwin, Earl Leofric and Earl Siward, all confirmed by oath and pledge of hands that after Edward's death they would receive me as lord. They also pledged that during their lifetimes, they would never seek in any way to prevent my succession to this country . . . Finally, Edward sent Harold himself to Normandy, that he might swear there in my presence what his father and the other aforesaid magnates had sworn in my absence. On his way to me he fell into the peril of captivity, from which I delivered him by the exercise of both prudence and force. He did homage to me and gave me pledge of hand concerning the English kingdom.

**Source B:** William of Malmesbury, writing in the early twelfth century, about the Battle of Hastings.

The Normans passed the whole night in confessing their sins, and received the communion of the Lord's body in the morning. Their infantry, with bows and arrows, formed the vanguard, while their cavalry, divided into wings, was placed in the rear. The Duke declared that God would favour his as being the righteous side, and called for his arms. Then the battle commenced on both sides, and was fought with great ardour, neither side giving ground during the greater part of the day.

William gave a signal to his troops to pretend to flee, and withdraw from the field. By means of this trick, the solid ranks of the English opened for the purpose of cutting down the fleeing enemy and thus brought upon itself their swift destruction. For the Normans, facing about, attacked them and compelled them to fly. In this manner, deceived by a stratagem, they met an honourable death; nor indeed were they at all without their own revenge, for, by frequently making a stand, they slaughtered their pursuers in heaps.

**Source C:** *Kingship and Unity*, G. W. S. Barrow, (1993).

By the end of King David's reign, a vast area of Scotland south of the Forth had been allocated to tenants (almost all newcomers) holding by military service. These men enjoyed the right to transmit their estates to their sons or other heirs by blood or family relationship. Even Moray in the far north was rapidly feudalised. Of even more lasting importance, however, were the burghs which were founded in almost every part of his kingdom outside the essentially highland area. Such an explosion of new ideas, policies and practices could hardly have happened within a single generation without a leader of exceptional energy and determination, backed up by a cohort of like-minded strangers wielding, or protected by, formidable military power.

**Source D:** *The New Penguin History of Scotland*, R. A. Houston and W. W. J. Knox (ed), 2001.

Scottish society was never fully "feudalised". The kindred-based ethos of pre-existing social patterns in Celtic Scotland blunted the hard edge and binding legalities of feudalism found elsewhere in Christendom. Also, Scottish lordship was strongly regional in nature. Substantial landowners often enjoyed heritable jurisdictions of their domains, which meant that most aspects of justice were the responsibility of the local lord rather than central government. Local justice may, as a result, have been more understanding of regional concerns than the more distant state was.

**Source E:** from an account of the Domesday Survey, written by Robert, Bishop of Hereford, one of the clergy brought to England by William.

William made a survey of all of England, of the lands in each of the counties. He ordered a survey of the possessions of each of the great lords, their lands, their houses, their men, both bond and free. He sought to know whether they lived in huts, or with their own houses or land: he sought to know the number of ploughs, horses and other animals. In particular, he ordered a survey of the payments due from each and every estate.

After these investigations, others were sent to visit unfamiliar counties to check the first description and to denounce any wrong-doers to the king. And the land was troubled with many calamities arising from the gathering of the royal taxes.

*[END OF SOURCES FOR SPECIAL TOPIC 1]*

### SPECIAL TOPIC 1: NORMAN CONQUEST AND EXPANSION 1050–1153

**Answer *all* of the following questions.**

*Marks*

1. How valuable is **Source A** as evidence of the justice of William's claim to the throne of England?
   *In reaching a conclusion you should refer to:*
   * *the origin and possible purpose of the source;*
   * *the content of the source;*
   * *recalled knowledge.*    **5**

2. How fully does **Source B** explain the Norman victory at Hastings?
   *Use the source and recalled knowledge.*    **6**

3. Compare the views expressed in **Sources C** and **D** about the development of feudalism in Scotland.
   *Compare the content overall and in detail.*    **5**

4. To what extent does **Source E** illustrate William's methods of ruling England?
   *Use the source and recalled knowledge.*    **6**

5. How successful were the Normans in establishing feudalism in England and Scotland?
   *Use **Sources C**, **D** and **E** and recalled knowledge.*    **8**

   **(30)**

*[END OF QUESTIONS ON SPECIAL TOPIC 1]*

### SPECIAL TOPIC 2: THE CRUSADES 1096–1204

**Study the sources below and then answer the questions which follow.**

**Source A:** An illumination from the 14th Century manuscript, Les Passages faites Outremer. In the picture Bishop Adhemar lifts the Holy Lance from its hiding place in the Church of St Peter in Antioch.

**Source B:** is from *Itinerarium Peregrinorum et Gesta Regis Ricardi*. It discusses the reasons for Philip's departure from the Third Crusade.

When things had thus been arranged after the surrender of Acre, toward the end of the month of July, a rumour circulated all at once through the army that the King of France wished to go home, and earnestly desired to prepare for his journey. How shameful was it for him to leave while the task was unfinished, when his duty was to lead and improve Christian men in the holy Crusade.

However, the French King claimed that illness had been the cause for his pilgrimage and that he had now fulfilled his vow as a Crusader as far as he could. King Richard demanded that the French King take an oath to keep faith and that he promise that he would not knowingly or maliciously trespass on Richard's land or the lands of his followers while Richard remained on Crusade.

How far the French King stood by this agreement and oath is known well enough to everyone. For, as soon as he re-entered his homeland, he stirred up the country and threw Normandy into disorder.

**Source C:** is from *Lionhearts, Saladin and Richard* by Geoffrey Regan.

Philip Augustus felt he also had reason enough to leave Outremer after the fall of Acre. Apart from the fact that Richard's presence only served to remind him how much he disliked the English king, there was also a major financial incentive to return to France. In the first place the Count of Flanders had died, giving him an opportunity to benefit from the deceased's extensive lands on the borders of France. Furthermore, since Richard was on Crusade and adding daily to his reputation as a Crusader, he would not be able to defend his land in Normandy and Aquitaine should Philip decide to settle any border disputes in his absence. Philip requested leave of absence sending four of his chief noblemen to explain to the Lionheart that ill health made it essential that they return to France . . . Richard was scornful of such an excuse.

**Source D:** is taken from the Itinerary of Richard I and describes the situation at Ascalon between Richard and the Duke of Burgundy.

After Richard had captured Ascalon, and was carefully rebuilding the walls of the city, a quarrel took place between him and the Duke of Burgundy. The Duke could not pay his men who were near mutiny, and asked Richard for a large sum of money for this purpose. However, on a former occasion, Richard had already lent the French an immense sum of money at Acre, which was to be repaid out of the ransom money from the captives. Therefore King Richard refused his application for money. It was because of this, and other causes of disagreement between the two men, that the Duke left Ascalon; and despite his inability to pay them, the French set out hastily with the Duke towards Acre.

**Source E:** *The Crusades,* W. B. Bartlett (1999)

Meanwhile, other negotiations had been taking place. Conrad had made his own approaches to Saladin through Reynald of Sidon. Saladin sought the advice of his council, wanting to know whether he should side with Conrad or Richard. They argued that he should support Richard, as he was unlikely to be in Outremer for too long. Saladin's double-dealings soon became public knowledge. Richard's representative, Humphrey of Toron, saw Al-Adil out hunting with Reynald and realised that other discussions were taking place. In addition, the Crusaders in Outremer were as disunited as ever and Richard's envoys were dismayed to discover that Conrad was still talking to Saladin. In particular, the presence of Balian of Ibelin among Conrad's entourage gave cause for concern. If such a prominent man and one much respected by the Franks was openly supporting Conrad, it suggested real problems ahead.

*[END OF SOURCES FOR SPECIAL TOPIC 2]*

### SPECIAL TOPIC 2: THE CRUSADES 1096–1204

**Answer *all* of the following questions.**

*Marks*

1. How useful is **Source A** as evidence of the significance for the Crusaders of the discovery of the Holy Lance?
   *In reaching a conclusion you should refer to:*
   * *the origin and possible purpose of the source;*
   * *the content of the source;*
   * *recalled knowledge.*　　　　5

2. Compare the views given in **Sources B** and **C** on the departure of Philip Augustus from the Third Crusade.
   *Compare the content overall and in detail.*　　　　5

3. To what extent does **Source D** illustrate the view that Richard I was a good soldier but a poor diplomat?
   *Use the source and recalled knowledge.*　　　　6

4. How fully do **Sources B**, **D** and **E** explain the reasons for the failure of the Third Crusade?
   *Use **Sources B**, **D** and **E** and recalled knowledge.*　　　　8

5. How important was the lack of unity among the leaders described in **Source E** in explaining the decline of the crusading ideal?
   *Use the source and recalled knowledge.*　　　　6

(30)

*[END OF QUESTIONS ON SPECIAL TOPIC 2]*

## OPTION B: EARLY MODERN HISTORY

### SPECIAL TOPIC 3: SCOTLAND 1689–1715

**Study the sources below and then answer the questions which follow.**

**Source A:** from P. H. Scott, *The Union of Scotland and England* (1979).

The Scottish Parliament turned to measures designed to restore Scottish trade from the effects of a century of neglect and discrimination. In 1695 it passed an Act for a company trading to Africa and the Indies. This was the Company of Scotland, which as the first of its ventures, decided to settle a colony at Darien. William, as King of Scotland, agreed to the Act and signed the Charter of the Company. As King of England, he was obliged to do all he could to sabotage and oppose the efforts of the Company.

When the Darien scheme failed, it was largely due to mismanagement and inadequate preparation. Many asked how a country could succeed when its own Head of State actively opposed its interests.

At this critical moment, when relations between the two countries were as bad as they had ever been, a dynastic accident offered a solution. The last child of Queen Anne died in 1700. In 1701, the English Parliament, without consultation with Scotland, passed the Act of Settlement, passing the succession after Anne to the Electress Sophia of Hanover.

**Source B:** from the Earl of Seafield's letters.

My reasons for joining with England on good terms were these: that the kingdom of England is a Protestant kingdom and that, therefore, the joining with them was a security for our religion. Secondly, England has trade and other advantages to give us, which no other kingdom could offer. Thirdly, England has freedom and liberty, and joining with them was the best way to secure that to us; and fourthly, I saw no other method for securing peace, the two kingdoms being in the same island, and foreign assistance was both dangerous to ourselves and England. Therefore, I was for the treaty.

**Source C:** from a petition from Stirling Town Council against the proposed union, 18th November 1706.

We desire that true peace and friendship be always cultivated with our neighbour England, upon just and honourable terms . . . Yet we judge that going into this Treaty will bring a burden of taxation upon this land, which freedom of trade will never repay . . . Scotland would still be under the regulations of the English in the Parliament of Britain, who may if they please discourage the most valuable branches of our trade, if we in any way are seen to interfere with their own. It will ruin our manufactories, our religion, laws and liberties.

As a result, one of the most ancient nations so long and so gloriously defended will be suppressed. Our parliament and all that is dear to us will be extinguished.

**Source D:** from William Ferguson, *Scotland's Relations with England* (1977).

The Equivalent, indeed, had a major part to play in getting members to favour the treaty . . . Part of it was earmarked to meet arrears of salaries and was later so used . . . It is not really possible to say how much money Queensberry made from the union, so tangled are the accounts, but certainly he obtained much more than the £12,000 sterling Seafield referred to.

The Equivalent was politically useful in other ways. The Squadrone was tricked into supporting the Union by a promise, later broken, that as nominees of the directors of the Company of Scotland, they would be allowed to handle that part of the Equivalent intended to compensate the shareholders.

**Source E:** from the House of Lords Journal, June 1713.

The Question is put to the House:

That permission be given to bring in a Bill, to end the Union; and for restoring each Kingdom to their Rights and Privileges as they had been at the time when the Union was first passed . . .

That charging Scotland with this Malt Tax, will be a violation of the 14th article of the Treaty of Union; by which it was clearly stated "that Scotland shall not be charged with any Malt Tax during this war;"

We must regard it as unjust, to make that part of the United Kingdom pay any part of this tax.

[END OF SOURCES FOR SPECIAL TOPIC 3]

## SPECIAL TOPIC 3: SCOTLAND 1689–1715

**Answer *all* of the following questions.**

*Marks*

1. To what extent does **Source A** show the problems which resulted from Scotland sharing the same monarch with England?
   *Use the source and recalled knowledge.*                                    **6**

2. Compare the attitudes towards the Union expressed in **Sources B** and **C**.
   *Compare the content overall and in detail.*                                 **5**

3. How adequately does **Source D** explain the importance of financial incentives in winning support for the Treaty of Union?
   *Use the source and recalled knowledge.*                                    **6**

4. How fully do **Sources A**, **B** and **D** explain why a majority of Scots MPs voted for Union?
   *Use **Sources A**, **B** and **D** and recalled knowledge.*                 **8**

5. How useful is **Source E** as evidence of discontent with the Union after 1707?
   *In reaching a conclusion you should refer to:*
   • *the origin and possible purpose of the source;*
   • *the content of the source;*
   • *recalled knowledge.*                                                       **5**

                                                                                **(30)**

[END OF QUESTIONS ON SPECIAL TOPIC 3]

**SPECIAL TOPIC 4: THE ATLANTIC SLAVE TRADE**

**Study the sources below and then answer the questions which follow.**

**Source A:** from David Northrup, *The Atlantic Slave Trade*, (2002)

In the eighteenth century, slavery came under mounting attack by philosophical and religious thinkers as well as by slave rebels. Antislavery societies sprang up in many Western countries. Ironically, it was in Great Britain, whose traders dominated the carrying of slaves across the Atlantic, that the largest and most influential abolitionist movement arose. Led by religious idealists—Quakers, Methodists and evangelical Anglicans—the British abolitionist movement also gained the support of a new industrial middle class, whose members identified slavery with outdated economic ideas. For both moral and economic reasons, these people supported the abolition of the Slave Trade as the first step toward ending slavery.

**Source B:** from a report issued by the London Abolition Committee, June 1795.

We have to inform our numerous friends, that the hostility which many in this country have shown from the use of West Indian produce, has given so much encouragement to the production and importation of East Indian sugar. We are of the opinion, while the Slave Trade continues, that a clear preference should be given to the East Indian sugar, as well as to all other substitutes for the produce of the West Indian Islands, particularly sugar, rum, cotton, coffee, cocoa and chocolate.

**Source C:** from a Petition of the merchants of Liverpool to the House of Commons, *c. 1788*.

We regard with real concern the attempts now being made to obtain a total abolition of the African Slave Trade. We humbly pray that our views may be heard against the abolition of this source of wealth. This should take place before the Honourable House shall make a decision upon a point which is so essential to the welfare of Liverpool in particular, and the landed interest of the kingdom in general. In our judgement, abolition must also do harm to the British manufacturers, must ruin the property of the English merchants in the West Indies, reduce the public revenue and damage the maritime strength of Great Britain.

**Source D:** from Petitions of the West Indian Traders of Bristol, May 1789.

It has been found with great exactness that the African and West India trade makes up at least three fifths of the commerce of the port of Bristol. If Wilberforce's Bill should pass into law, the decline of the trade of Bristol must inevitably follow, with the ruin of thousands . . .

Many of our Master Bakers and bread shops depend chiefly for employment on the great number of ships fitted out in Bristol and from the great number of people to be fed on board these ships during a long voyage. Many of the vessels are fitted out by the local drapers, grocers, tailors, and other tradesmen. A very considerable part of the various manufactures that we, the petitioners, produce are adapted to the African trade and are not saleable in any other market . . .

The welfare of the West Indian Islands, and the commerce and revenue of the United Kingdom so essentially depend on the slave trade being carried on.

**Source E:** from Peter J. Kitson, *Slavery, Abolition and Emancipation* (1999)

External circumstances were to affect the cause of abolition at home. In 1792 the French Revolution set out on a more extreme and threatening direction. One of the consequences of this was the encouragement of revolutionary expectations in the French colonies. In 1791 the mulattos of St Domingue began a revolt which was followed by a full-scale slave uprising. The effect of these events was to frighten opinion at home concerning any attempts to criticise the present constitutional arrangements. The defenders of the trade in the debates of 1792 repeatedly blamed the St Domingue uprising on the activities of the French and British abolitionists. Many of those who had hitherto supported abolition now became nervous at the turn which events were taking.

*[END OF SOURCES FOR SPECIAL TOPIC 4]*

## SPECIAL TOPIC 4: THE ATLANTIC SLAVE TRADE

**Answer *all* of the following questions.**

*Marks*

1. To what extent does **Source A** identify the reasons for the campaign to abolish the Slave Trade?
   *Use the source and recalled knowledge.*                                                      **6**

2. How useful is **Source B** as evidence of the activities of the Abolitionists?
   *In reaching a conclusion you should refer to:*
   * *the origin and possible purpose of the source;*
   * *the content of the source;*
   * *recalled knowledge.*                                                                       **5**

3. To what extent does **Source C** illustrate the arguments used by supporters of the Slave Trade?
   *Use the source and recalled knowledge.*                                                      **6**

4. How far do **Sources C** and **D** agree on the likely effects of the abolition of the Slave Trade?
   *Compare the content overall and in detail.*                                                  **5**

5. How fully do **Sources B**, **C** and **E** reflect the issues in the debate over the abolition of the Slave Trade?
   *Use **Sources B**, **C** and **E** and recalled knowledge.*                                  **8**
   **(30)**

*[END OF QUESTIONS ON SPECIAL TOPIC 4]*

## SPECIAL TOPIC 5: THE AMERICAN REVOLUTION

**Study the sources below and then answer the questions which follow.**

**Source A:** from a speech by General Conway in the Parliamentary debate on the Coercive Acts, 1774.

It is my sincere opinion that we are the aggressors and not the colonies. We have irritated and forced laws upon them for these six or seven years past. We have enacted such a variety of laws and new taxes and we have refused to repeal the trifling duty on tea. All these things have served no other purpose but to distress and confuse the colonists. I think the Americans have done no more than every British subject would do, where laws are imposed against their will.

**Source B:** from a letter by John Adams reflecting on the Boston Tea Party, 1773.

The question is whether the destruction of this tea was necessary. I believe it was—absolutely and indispensably so. The Governor would not allow the tea to be sent back. So there was no other alternative but to destroy it or let it be landed. To let it be landed, would be giving up the principle of taxation by Parliamentary authority, against which the Continent has struggled for 10 years. It would destroy all our efforts for the last 10 years and force us and our descendants forever to accept burdens and indignities, desolation and oppression, poverty and servitude.

**Source C:** from a letter from a Virginian to a friend in Scotland, January, 1776.

Tears fill my eyes when I think of this once happy land of liberty. All is anarchy and confusion . . . We are all in arms . . . The sound of war echoes from north to south. There are armed men everywhere. May God put a speedy and happy end to this grand and important contest between the mother and her children. The colonies do not wish to be independent; they only deny the right of taxation in Parliament. Our Assemblies would freely grant the King whatever he asks of us, provided Parliament plays no part in the process . . .

**Source D:** from a letter from George Washington to Marquis de Lafayette, September 1781.

But my dear Marquis, I am distressed beyond expression to know what is become of the Count De Grasse. I fear the English fleet, by occupying the Chesapeake . . . would frustrate all our excellent chances of success in that area.

If the retreat of Lord Cornwallis by water is cut off by the arrival of either of the French fleets, I am confident you will do all in your power to prevent his escape by land. May that great good fortune be reserved for you!

You see how critically important the present moment is. For my own part, I am determined to persist with my present plan, unless some unavoidable and impossible obstacles are thrown in our way.

**Source E:** from D. Higginbotham and J. R. Pole (eds), *A Companion to the American Revolution*, (2000).

It was a great advantage to Americans to be fighting on their own soil and to be more flexible in their military operations than their opponents. They did not fight a massive guerrilla war, but nonetheless they resorted advantageously at times to winter campaigning and night attacks. They effectively employed backwoods riflemen, light infantry and militia in harassing the British flanks, interrupting communication and supply routes, and raiding isolated posts.

British leaders were increasingly frustrated by waging a war 3,000 miles from home against an armed population spread over enormous stretches of territory. It was disheartening to seize, somewhere along the way, every single American urban centre, including the capital city of Philadelphia, and have nothing to show for it other than the possession of property, for America had no vital strategic centre.

*[END OF SOURCES FOR SPECIAL TOPIC 5]*

## SPECIAL TOPIC 5: THE AMERICAN REVOLUTION

**Answer *all* of the following questions.**

*Marks*

1. How accurately does **Source A** identify the causes of the conflict between Britain and her American Colonies?
   *Use the source and recalled knowledge.*    **6**

2. To what extent does **Source B** agree with the explanation in **Source A** of the actions of the Colonists?
   *Compare the content overall and in detail.*    **5**

3. How typical is **Source C** of the attitude of the Colonists to Britain by 1776?
   *Use the source and recalled knowledge.*    **6**

4. How useful is **Source D** as evidence of the importance of foreign help to the Colonists in the War of Independence?
   *In reaching a conclusion you should refer to:*
   * *the origin and possible purpose of the source;*
   * *the content of the source;*
   * *recalled knowledge.*    **5**

5. How fully do **Sources C**, **D** and **E** explain the reasons for Colonial victory in the war?
   *Use **Sources C**, **D** and **E** and recalled knowledge.*    **8**

   **(30)**

*[END OF QUESTIONS ON SPECIAL TOPIC 5]*

## OPTION C: LATER MODERN HISTORY

### SPECIAL TOPIC 6: PATTERNS OF MIGRATION: SCOTLAND 1830s–1930s

**Study the sources below and then answer the questions which follow.**

**Source A:** from G. C. Lewis, *Inquiry into the State of the Irish Poor in Great Britain,* (1836)

In all the towns of England and Scotland where the Irish have settled, they inhabit the cheapest dwellings, and thus they are crowded into the poorest, dampest, dirtiest, most unhealthy parts of the town. An Irish family usually occupies one room, or at most two rooms; and frequently, in addition to their own numbers, they take in a single man or woman, or a widow with children, as lodgers. Altogether, the Irish differ more from the native Scots in their living arrangements than in any other way. They appear to be scarcely aware of the problems arising from the crowding of large numbers into small spaces.

**Source B:** from a report into Catholic schools in Scotland, by a Government Inspector, 1859.

The evening schools attended by Irish immigrant girls are the salvation of many of them who are exposed to the bad influences in both factories and streets of our large cities. When these night schools are in the hands of the religious teachers then they produce the most satisfactory results. On many a wet evening, I have seen these schoolrooms crowded with factory girls tidily dressed and working hard to improve their prospects in life through education. At the end of the school time, these girls would go to their prayers in the church. I was assured by the priest that many of them attended religious services throughout the week, and were of exemplary character in their lives.

The Catholic Church is attempting to help these poor girls to better themselves in life through education and other means.

**Source C:** from William Ferguson, *Scotland, 1689 to the Present* (1968).

The developing economy of Scotland proved very attractive to the poverty-stricken Irish. In some ways they were an economic asset, providing a hard-working, mobile force of unskilled labour. Gangs of Irish "navvies" did excellent work in all sorts of construction projects, particularly canal and railway building. They also provided a supply of seasonal labourers.

However, they also acted as cut-price labour in the mines, where they were frequently employed as strike-breakers, and they added to the miseries of the hand-loom weavers by swamping that already overcrowded trade with cheap labour. Economic rivalry gave rise to bitter resentment, especially in the coalfields of Lanarkshire, although seasonal harvesters, both Highland and Lowland, also had grievances about losing work to the Irish workers.

**Source D:** from M. Harper, *Adventurers and Exiles; The Great Scottish Exodus* (2003).

Scots were attracted overseas for a variety of economic, social and cultural reasons. The promise of independence through land ownership was a powerful attraction, particularly to those whose security and prospects had been reduced by the changes in farming in Scotland. For many, the expected neighbourliness, co-operation and familiarity of an established Scottish settlement were incentives just as important as material gain and the absence of domineering landlords. However, the most effective encouragement to emigrate came undoubtedly from a satisfied emigrant's letter home. For emigrants who lacked overseas contacts, professional emigration agents might influence their decisions.

**Source E:** extract from a letter written by a Scottish emigrant living in Canada, 1889.

If truth be told, many who come out here live out a miserable existence. The people who live in the town of Red Deer are sleepy, with no "go" in them, and other places are no better, some even worse. In Edmonton, the price of property is very high. Our idea in coming to this country was to take up the free land for farming but everything is so different as to how it is described in the agents' pamphlets.

For instance, we are told that splendid homesteads can be had within a mile or two of the railway for 10 dollars. In plain English, this is a downright lie. The *nearest* homestead land I could get was about 35 miles from the railway, and to get land that was worth having, I had to go about 60 to 80 miles from the town and railway. This is the last place on earth that I would care to remain in.

*[END OF SOURCES FOR SPECIAL TOPIC 6]*

### SPECIAL TOPIC 6: PATTERNS OF MIGRATION: SCOTLAND 1830s–1930s

**Answer *all* of the following questions.**

*Marks*

1. How useful is **Source A** as evidence of the living conditions of Irish immigrants in Scotland in the first half of the nineteenth century?
   *In reaching a conclusion you should refer to:*
   • *the origin and possible purpose of the source;*
   • *the content of the source;*
   • *recalled knowledge.*    **5**

2. How fully does **Source B** describe the importance of the Catholic Church in the lives of Irish immigrants in Scotland?
   *Use the source and recalled knowledge.*    **6**

3. Why did anti-Irish feeling develop among native Scots during the period 1830s–1930s?
   *Use **Sources A**, **B** and **C** and recalled knowledge.*    **8**

4. How typical of the experiences of emigrant Scots are the views expressed in **Source E**?
   *Use the source and recalled knowledge.*    **6**

5. To what extent does the evidence in **Source D** support the views in **Source E** on the experiences of Scottish emigrants overseas?
   *Compare the content overall and in detail.*    **5**

   **(30)**

*[END OF QUESTIONS ON SPECIAL TOPIC 6]*

## SPECIAL TOPIC 7: APPEASEMENT AND THE ROAD TO WAR, TO 1939

**Study the sources below and then answer the questions which follow.**

**Source A:** from the review by the Chiefs of Staff of British Armed Forces, July 1936, following the remilitarisation of the Rhineland.

Our military backwardness has placed us in a very weak position.

The present situation dictates a policy towards reaching an understanding with Germany. This will postpone the danger of German aggression against any vital interest of ours. It is important that we do this because of the extreme weakness of France, the possibility of an understanding between Germany and Japan and even Italy, and the huge risks to which a direct attack upon Great Britain would expose the Empire.

**Source B:** from a speech by Winston Churchill in the House of Commons, 14th March, 1938.

The seriousness of the events of March 12th (the German annexation of Austria) should be obvious. Europe is faced with a programme of aggression, calculated and timed, unfolding stage by stage. There is only one choice open, not only to us but to other countries. We can either submit like Austria, or else take effective measures while time remains, to head off the danger. If it cannot be avoided we must cope with it.

If we go on waiting upon events, how much shall we throw away of resources now available for our security and the maintenance of peace? How many friends and possible allies will be lost? Where are we going to be two years from now? The German army will certainly be much larger than the French army. Will all the small nations have left the League of Nations and be looking towards the ever-growing power of the Nazi system, to make the best terms that they can for themselves?

**Source C:** from a letter from the Conservative MP, Thomas Moore, to the national newspaper, *The Times*, 17th March 1938.

If the Austrian people had not welcomed this union, violence and bloodshed would have occurred. So far, there has been none, and this proves the strong desire of the two nations to bring about the Anschluss of which they have been so long deprived by the leading European powers. Austria now has free markets for her raw materials and manufactured goods but, more important still, she is no longer a source of conflict in international relations.

Let us therefore consider the benefits for Austria and Europe before laying the blame for a development which in the end may prove a decisive factor in European appeasement.

**Source D:** from the leading article in *The Scotsman* newspaper, 1st October 1938.

All the world is agreed that, but for the determination of the British Prime Minister, Europe would have been plunged into a horrible, soul-destroying war that would have killed millions, laid great cities waste, impoverished the nations, and sown the fresh seeds of bitterness and hostility in international relations. We should be very grateful to the statesmen who have saved Europe from such a calamity.

The statesmen of the Western democracies and of the two leading Fascist states have confronted each other over the abyss of war. But now, there is reason for hope in the remarkable declaration signed yesterday by Mr. Chamberlain and Herr Hitler at Munich.

It is true that Germany has given too many reasons for distrust, and her methods are violent, and her ambitions suspect. But, except on a basis of trust, we cannot remove fear and suspicion from international relations, or even begin to lay the foundations of a lasting world peace. Mr. Chamberlain's method of approach is the only way of progress. May he have the strength and support to carry it on to complete the process.

**Source E:** from *The Shadow of the Bomber*, U. Biailer, 1980.

The government's preoccupation with aerial warfare, and specifically with the danger of bombing, made it necessary that the highest priority be given to the means required to counter an air attack on Britain. Throughout the long debate on rearmament and strategy during the latter half of the 1930s, many experts argued this would undermine Britain's ability to use land forces in Europe. This debate was not resolved until December 1937. It was then decided that spending on the Army would be calculated on the assumption that British forces would not have to fight a land war in Europe.

*[END OF SOURCES FOR SPECIAL TOPIC 7]*

### SPECIAL TOPIC 7: APPEASEMENT AND THE ROAD TO WAR, TO 1939

**Answer *all* of the following questions.**

*Marks*

1. How useful is **Source A** as evidence of British concern following Germany's remilitarisation of the Rhineland in 1936?
   *In reaching a conclusion you should refer to:*
   * *the origin and possible purpose of the source;*
   * *the content of the source;*
   * *recalled knowledge.*

   5

2. How adequately does **Source B** explain the dangers facing Britain after the Anschluss?
   *Use the source and recalled knowledge.*

   6

3. Compare the views on the Anschluss expressed in **Sources B** and **C**.
   *Compare the content overall and in detail.*

   5

4. To what extent do the views expressed in **Source D** reflect British reaction to the Munich Agreement?
   *Use the source and recalled knowledge.*

   6

5. How fully do **Sources A**, **D** and **E** explain why the British government adopted the policy of appeasement?
   *Use **Sources A**, **D** and **E** and recalled knowledge.*

   8

   **(30)**

*[END OF QUESTIONS ON SPECIAL TOPIC 7]*

**SPECIAL TOPIC 8: THE ORIGINS AND DEVELOPMENT OF THE COLD WAR 1945–1985**

**Study the sources below and then answer the questions which follow.**

**Source A:** from an official statement by the Soviet Government, 30 October, 1956.

The course of events has shown that the working people of Hungary correctly raise the question of the necessity of eliminating serious shortcomings in their country.

However, forces of reaction and counter revolution are trying to take advantage of the discontent of part of the working people. They are trying to undermine the foundations of the people's democratic order in Hungary and to restore the old landlord and capitalist order.

The Soviet Government and all the Soviet people deeply regret that the development of events in Hungary has led to bloodshed. On the request of the Hungarian People's Government, the Soviet Government consented to the entry into Budapest of the Soviet Army units to assist the Hungarian People's Army and the Hungarian authorities to establish order in the city.

**Source B:** from Imry Nagy: Last Message (November 4, 1956).

This fight is the fight for freedom by the Hungarian people against the Russian intervention, and it is possible that I shall only be able to stay at my post for one or two hours. The whole world will see how the Russian armed forces, contrary to all treaties and conventions, are crushing the resistance of the Hungarian people. They will also see how they are kidnapping the Prime Minister of a country which is a Member of the United Nations, taking him from his capital. It cannot be doubted at all that this is the most brutal form of intervention.

I ask that our leaders should turn to all the peoples of the world for help and explain that today it is Hungary and tomorrow, or the day after tomorrow, it will be the turn of other countries. The imperialism of Moscow does not recognise borders, and is only trying to play for time.

**Source C:** from a pamphlet issued by the German Democratic Republic entitled *"What You Should Know About the Wall"*, issued in 1962.

We no longer wanted to stand by passively and see how doctors, engineers, and skilled workers were persuaded by corrupt and unworthy methods to give up their secure existence in the GDR and work in West Germany or West Berlin. These and other tricks cost the GDR annual losses amounting to 3·5 thousand million marks.

But we prevented something much more important with the Wall—West Berlin could have become the starting point for military conflict. The measures we introduced on 13 August in conjunction with the Warsaw Treaty states have cooled off a number of hotheads in Bonn and Berlin.

**Source D:** from Paul Kennedy, *The Rise and Fall of the Great Powers* (1988).

In 1955, the USSR was mass-producing a medium-range ballistic missile (the SS-3). By 1957, it had fired an intercontinental ballistic missile over a range of five thousand miles, using the same rocket engine which shot *Sputnik*, the earth's first artificial satellite, into orbit in October of the same year.

Shocked by these Russian advances, and by the implication that both US cities and US bomber forces might be vulnerable to a sudden Soviet strike, Washington committed massive resources to its own intercontinental ballistic missiles in order to close what was predictably termed "the missile gap". But the nuclear arms race was not confined to such systems. From 1960 onward, each side was also developing a wide variety of other weapons.

**Source E:** from S. J. Ball, *The Cold War: An International History 1947–1991* (1998)

A group set up by President Kennedy concluded that "stronger US actions were needed to assist the Vietnamese against Communism in the South East Asia region". These included expanding the ARVN (Army of the Republic of Vietnam), supplying more US aid and sending US advisers to directly participate in anti-guerrilla warfare ... At the end of 1961 an American government report concluded: "the United States must decide how it will cope with Khrushchev's 'wars of liberation' which are really wars of guerrilla aggression. This is a new and dangerous Communist technique which bypasses our traditional and military responses." Faced with this supposed threat, Kennedy expanded the numbers of US advisers from 400 to 16,000.

*[END OF SOURCES FOR SPECIAL TOPIC 8]*

### SPECIAL TOPIC 8: THE ORIGINS AND DEVELOPMENT OF THE COLD WAR 1945–1985

**Answer *all* of the following questions.**

*Marks*

1. How fully does **Source A** explain the reasons for Soviet intervention in Hungary in 1956?
   *Use the source and recalled knowledge.*    **6**

2. Compare the views on events in Hungary in 1956 expressed in **Sources A** and **B**.
   *Compare the content overall and in detail.*    **5**

3. How useful is **Source C** as evidence of East Germany's reasons for constructing the Berlin Wall in 1961?
   *In reaching a conclusion you should refer to:*
   * *the origin and possible purpose of the source;*
   * *the content of the source;*
   * *recalled knowledge.*    **5**

4. To what extent does **Source D** illustrate the development of the Arms Race?
   *Use the source and recalled knowledge.*    **6**

5. How fully do **Sources C**, **D** and **E** explain the issues which divided the superpowers in the 1950s and 1960s?
   *Use **Sources C**, **D** and **E** and recalled knowledge.*    **8**

   **(30)**

*[END OF QUESTIONS ON SPECIAL TOPIC 8]*

**SPECIAL TOPIC 9: IRELAND 1900–1985: A DIVIDED IDENTITY**

**Study the sources below and then answer the questions which follow.**

**Source A:** John Redmond, addressing an Irish Volunteer Parade in County Wicklow, 20th September 1914.

The duty of the men of Ireland is twofold. Their duty is, at all costs, to defend the shores of Ireland against foreign invasion. More than that, they must ensure that Irish courage proves itself on the battlefield as it has always proved itself in the past.

The interests of Ireland—of the whole of Ireland—are at stake in this war. The war is undertaken in defence of the highest principles of religion and morality and right. It would be a disgrace for ever if young Ireland confined its efforts to remaining at home to defend the shores of Ireland from an unlikely invasion, and failed in its duty of showing the gallantry and courage which has distinguished our race through all its history.

I say to you, therefore, "Go on drilling and making yourselves fit and ready for the work, and then behave like men, not only in Ireland itself, but wherever the firing line extends."

**Source B:** From an open letter by the Bishop of Limerick, the Most Rev. Dr. O'Dwyer, (November 1915).

It is very probable that these poor Connacht peasants know little or nothing of the meaning of the war. Their blood is not stirred by the memories of German aggression, and they have no burning desire to die for Serbia. They would much prefer to be allowed to till their own potato gardens in peace in Connemara. Their view is that they are not ready to die for England. Why should they? What have they or their ancestors ever got from England that they should die for her? Mr. Redmond will say "A Home Rule Act is on the statute book". But any intelligent Irishman will say "An Illusion of Home Rule" which will never come into operation. This war may be just or unjust, but any fair-minded man will admit that it is England's war, not Ireland's.

**Source C:** from F. S. L. Lyons, *Ireland since the Famine* (1973).

Two lorry loads of Auxiliaries . . . were slowed down by a trick and as the police climbed down from them they came under heavy fire; only one man survived. The very next day, another ambush only a few miles from Cork city caused more Auxiliaries casualties. That night Auxiliaries and Black and Tans poured in to the town, looting, wrecking, drinking and burning—burning to such effect, indeed, that a large part of the centre of the city was completely destroyed. The fire brigade was deliberately obstructed as they sought to bring the flames under control. The Auxiliaries made their own comment on the affair when they swaggered about the streets of Dublin with burnt corks in their caps.

**Source D:** from *The Twelve Apostles*, by D. Figgis. The author is describing a meeting with Michael Collins which he attended at the beginning of the Anglo-Irish War, 1919.

Michael Collins rose. As usual, he swept aside all pretences, and said that the announcement to use force had been written by him, and that the decision to make it had been made not by Sinn Fein but by the Irish Volunteers. He spoke more strongly, saying that the sooner fighting was forced and a general state of disorder created, the better it would be for the country. Ireland was likely to get more out of the state of general disorder than from a continuance of the situation as it then stood. The proper people to make decisions of that kind were ready to face the British military, and were resolved to force the issue, and they were not put off by weaklings and cowards. He accepted full responsibility for the announcement. He told the meeting with forceful honesty that he held them in no opinion at all; that, in fact, they were only summoned to confirm that the proper people had decided.

**Source E:** Joint Statement by Irish bishops, October 1922.

A section of the community, refusing to acknowledge the government set up by the nation, has chosen to attack their own country, as if she were a foreign power. Forgetting, apparently, that a dead nation cannot be free, they have deliberately set out to make our motherland, as far as they could, a heap of ruins. They have wrecked Ireland from end to end, burning and destroying national property of enormous value, breaking roads, bridges and railways, seeking by this blockade to starve the people . . . They carry on what they call a war but which, in the absence of any authority to justify it, is morally only a system of murder and assassination of the National forces. It must not be forgotten that killing in an unjust war is as much murder before God as if there was no war.

*[END OF SOURCES FOR SPECIAL TOPIC 9]*

### SPECIAL TOPIC 9: IRELAND 1900–1985: A DIVIDED IDENTITY

**Answer *all* of the following questions.**

*Marks*

1. How useful is **Source A** as evidence of Irish opinion on involvement in the First World War?
   *In reaching a conclusion you should refer to:*
   * *the origin and possible purpose of the source;*
   * *the content of the source;*
   * *recalled knowledge.*                                                          5

2. Compare the views expressed in **Sources A** and **B** on Irish support for Britain and the First World War.
   *Compare the content overall and in detail.*                                     5

3. How fully does **Source C** illustrate the methods used by both sides during the Anglo-Irish War?
   *Use the source and recalled knowledge.*                                         6

4. How much support was there at the time for the views expressed by the Irish bishops in **Source E**.
   *Use the source and recalled knowledge.*                                         6

5. How fully do **Sources B, D** and **E** explain the causes of division and conflict in Ireland during the period 1912–1922?
   *Use **Sources B**, **D** and **E** and recalled knowledge.*                      8

   (30)

*[END OF QUESTIONS ON SPECIAL TOPIC 9]*

*[END OF QUESTION PAPER]*

[BLANK PAGE]

[BLANK PAGE]

# X044/301

NATIONAL
QUALIFICATIONS
2009

TUESDAY, 2 JUNE
9.00 AM – 10.20 AM

HISTORY
HIGHER
Paper 1

Answer questions on **one** Option only.

Take particular care to show clearly the Option chosen. On the **front** of the answer book, **in the top right-hand corner**, write A or B or C.

Within the Option chosen, answer **two** questions, one from Historical Study: Scottish and British and one from Historical Study: European and World.

All questions are worth 20 marks.

[BLANK PAGE]

## OPTION A: MEDIEVAL HISTORY

**Answer TWO questions, one from Historical Study: Scottish and British and one from Historical Study: European and World**

### Historical Study: Scottish and British

**Medieval Society**

1. "Brutal, poor and without hope." How accurate is this view of the lives of peasants during the Middle Ages?

2. To what extent was the secular church more important than the regular church in the Middle Ages?

3. How important were towns to medieval society in England and Scotland?

4. How far can it be argued that David I was a successful feudal monarch?

5. "Henry II's greatest achievement was the establishment of a new justice system in England." How accurate is this statement?

### Historical Study: European and World

**EITHER**

**Nation and King**

6. To what extent were his failures in foreign policy the cause of baronial revolt against King John?

7. How important a contribution did William Wallace make to Scotland's eventual victory in the Scottish Wars of Independence?

8. How successful was Philip II in expanding royal power in France?

9. How far does the effective leadership of Louis IX explain the lack of baronial opposition to his attempts to strengthen the French monarchy?

**OR**

**Crisis of Authority**

10. "English success in the Hundred Years' War up to 1421 was due almost entirely to French weaknesses." How accurate is this statement?

11. To what extent was the Peasants' Revolt caused by a desire to end serfdom?

12. To what extent were the long-term consequences of the Black Death beneficial to Europe?

13. How successful was the Conciliar Movement in limiting the authority of the Papacy in Europe?

## OPTION B:  EARLY MODERN HISTORY

**Answer TWO questions, one from Historical Study:  Scottish and British
and one from Historical Study:  European and World**

### Historical Study:  Scottish and British

**EITHER**

**Scotland in the Age of the Reformation 1542–1603**

1. To what extent was Scotland dominated by France in the period 1542–1560?

2. How important was the role of John Knox in bringing about the Reformation in Scotland?

3. "A Catholic Queen in a Protestant land."  How important was religion as a reason for Mary Queen of Scots losing her throne?

4. How significant was the impact of the Reformation on Scotland by 1603?

5. How successfully had James VI established his authority over Scotland by 1603?

**OR**

**Scotland and England in the Century of Revolutions 1603–1702**

6. "Here I sit and govern with my pen."  How justified is this view of James VI and I's control of Scotland after 1603?

7. How important was foreign policy as a source of disagreement between James VI and I and his English Parliament?

8. To what extent was Charles I to blame for the outbreak of civil war in England?

9. How successful was Cromwell in his attempts to rule by constitutional means?

10. To what extent was the revolutionary settlement of 1688–1689 a successful compromise?

## Historical Study:  European and World

**EITHER**

### Royal Authority in 17th and 18th Century Europe

**11.** To what extent did Louis XIV establish absolute authority over France?

**12.** How successfully did Louis XIV deal with the religious challenges which faced him?

**13.** How far did the reforms introduced by Frederick II of Prussia improve the lives of his subjects?

**14.** To what extent was Joseph II successful in his efforts to introduce enlightened reforms in Austria?

**OR**

### The French Revolution:  The Emergence of the Citizen State

**15.** How important were economic problems in weakening the authority of the Ancien Regime?

**16.** To what extent was Louis XVI responsible for the failure of the constitutional monarchy of France?

**17.** "France became ungovernable during the Reign of Terror 1793–1794."  How justified is this view?

**18.** How far did the French people benefit from the effects of the Revolution by 1799?

**[Turn over**

## OPTION C:  LATER MODERN HISTORY

**Answer TWO questions, one from Historical Study:  Scottish and British
and one from Historical Study:  European and World**

### Historical Study:  Scottish and British

**Britain 1850s–1979**

1. "By 1928, Britain was a fully democratic country."  How accurate is this view?

2. How important were the trade unions in the growth of the Labour Party by 1906?

3. "Between 1931 and 1939, the British people suffered severe economic hardship."  How accurate is this statement?

4. How significant an impact did the welfare reforms of the Labour Government 1945–1951 have on the lives of the British people?

5. **Either**

   (a) "Urbanisation brought more problems than benefits to the lives of the Scottish people between 1880 and 1939."  How accurate is this view?

   **Or**

   (b) How far had Scotland developed its own political identity by 1979?

**Historical Study: European and World**

**EITHER**

**The Growth of Nationalism**

*Germany*

6. How important were economic factors in the growth of national feeling in Germany during the period 1815 to 1850?

7. How important was the role of Prussia in the achievement of German unification by 1871?

8. "Hitler's promise of a better future for the German people was the most important reason for the growth in support for the Nazis up to 1933." How accurate is this view?

9. To what extent was Nazi control of Germany from 1933 to 1939 due to the popularity of their policies?

*Italy*

10. How important were economic factors in the growth of national feeling in Italy during the period 1815 to 1850?

11. How important was the role of Piedmont in the achievement of Italian unification by 1871?

12. "Mussolini's promise of a better future for the Italian people was the most important reason for the growth in support for the Fascists up to 1922." How accurate is this view?

13. To what extent was Fascist control of Italy from 1922 to 1939 due to the popularity of their policies?

**[Turn over for The Large Scale State on *Page eight***

OR

**The Large Scale State**

*The USA*

14. To what extent was the increase in hostility towards immigrants in the USA during the 1920s due to fear of revolution?

15. To what extent was the economic boom of the 1920s caused by the development of mass production methods?

16. "The economic recovery of the 1930s can be explained entirely by the effects of the New Deal." How accurate is this view?

17. How successful were the black radical protest movements of the 1960s in achieving their aims?

*Russia*

18. How important was military power in maintaining the Tsarist state up to 1905?

19. "The power of the Tsarist state was relatively unchanged after the 1905 Revolution." How accurate is this view?

20. To what extent was the seizure of power by the Bolsheviks in October 1917 due to the failings of the Provisional Government?

21. How secure was the Bolsheviks' hold on power by 1921?

*[END OF QUESTION PAPER]*

# X044/302

NATIONAL
QUALIFICATIONS
2009

TUESDAY, 2 JUNE
10.40 AM – 12.05 PM

HISTORY
HIGHER
Paper 2

Answer questions on only **one** Special Topic.

Take particular care to show clearly the Special Topic chosen. On the **front** of the answer book, **in the top right-hand corner**, write the number of the Special Topic.

You are expected to use background knowledge appropriately in answering source-based questions.

Marks may be deducted for bad spelling and bad punctuation, and for writing that is difficult to read.

Some sources have been adapted or translated.

**[BLANK PAGE]**

## OPTION A: MEDIEVAL HISTORY

### SPECIAL TOPIC 1: NORMAN CONQUEST AND EXPANSION 1050–1153

**Study the sources below and then answer the questions which follow.**

**Source A:** The Battle of Hastings described in the Anglo-Saxon Chronicle, c. 1085.

Therefore King Harold at once, and in great haste, marched with his army to London. Although he well knew that some of the bravest Englishmen had fallen in the two former battles, and that one half of his army had not yet arrived, he did not hesitate to advance with all speed into Sussex against his enemies. On Saturday 14 October, before a third of his army was in order for fighting, he joined battle nine miles from Hastings, where his foes had built a castle. As the English were drawn up in a narrow place, many retired from the ranks, and very few remained true to him. At last, after great slaughter on both sides, about twilight the King, alas, fell. There were slain also Earl Gyrth and his brother, Earl Leofwine, and nearly all the magnates of England.

**Source B:** from the Ecclesiastical History of Orderic Vitalis, written between 1114 and 1141.

After the King's return from Normandy in 1068, he was at great pains to appease everyone. Every city and district which he had visited in person or occupied with his garrison obeyed his will. But in the marches of his kingdom, to the west and north, the inhabitants were still barbarous, and had only obeyed the English king in the time of Edward and his predecessors when it suited them. Exeter was the first town to fight for liberty, but it was defeated by the valiant forces that fiercely assaulted it.

The king commanded the leading citizens to swear fealty to him. They replied, "We will neither swear fealty nor admit him within our walls. But we will pay tribute to him according to ancient custom." The king replied, "It is not my custom to have subjects on such terms". He then marched on them in force and for the first time called out Englishmen to his army.

Finally, the citizens were compelled to take wiser counsel and humbly plead for pardon.

**Source C:** from the Ecclesiastical History of Orderic Vitalis, written between about 1114 and 1141.

But meanwhile the English were groaning under the Norman yoke, and suffering oppressions from the proud lords who ignored the commands of the king. The petty lords who were guarding the castles oppressed all the native inhabitants of high and low degree, and heaped shameful burdens on them. For Bishop Odo and William fitz Osbern, the king's vice regents, were so swollen with pride that they would not deign to hear the reasonable plea of the English or give them impartial judgement. When their men at arms were guilty of crimes such as plunder and rape, they protected them by force, and treated even more cruelly all those who complained of the cruel wrongs they suffered.

**Source D:** from Ian D Whyte, *Scotland before the Industrial Revolution* (1995).

In Scotland, Norman influence arrived peacefully through the deliberate policies of the Scottish Kings. Feudalism was imported gradually in a fully developed form. In practice, many aspects of eleventh century Scottish society, notably tenure, food renders and military service were already essentially feudal. It is doubtful if the bulk of the population noticed much difference with the transition from Celtic to feudal lordship.

It was not the case of Celtic traditions and institutions being replaced by Norman ones so much as the two blending and interacting. Scottish kings in the twelfth and thirteenth centuries were careful to strike a balance between continuity and change. Many developments, such as the spread of the parish system, involved standardising and improving existing structures which had previously developed in a piecemeal manner.

**Source E:** from B. Golding, *Conquest and Colonisation* (2001).

Eadmer of Canterbury, writing at the beginning of the twelfth century, maintained that William had brought from Normandy a heritage of tight secular control over the Church, which he then successfully imposed on its English counterpart. There can be no doubt that William I took an active interest in the affairs of the Anglo-Norman Church, or that William Rufus was equally forceful, if less diplomatic. Yet, when we look at the post-Conquest church, it is hard to evaluate what developments were directly attributable to the Normans. By introducing bishops and abbots from Normandy and beyond, William may have accelerated the pace of change, but he did not alter direction. Reform was already in the air before 1066, but in many aspects post conquest reform was archaic, in the light of new ideas current at the Roman Curia.

*[END OF SOURCES FOR SPECIAL TOPIC 1]*

**SPECIAL TOPIC 1: NORMAN CONQUEST AND EXPANSION 1050–1153**

**Answer *all* of the following questions.**

*Marks*

1. How fully does **Source A** explain the defeat of the English forces at the battle of Hastings?
   *Use the source and recalled knowledge.*
   **6**

2. How valuable is **Source B** as evidence of the nature of William's control of England immediately after the battle of Hastings?
   *In reaching a conclusion you should refer to:*
   • *the origin and possible purpose of the source;*
   • *the content of the source;*
   • *recalled knowledge.*
   **5**

3. Compare the views expressed in **Source C** and **Source D** about the influence of the Normans on English and Scottish society.
   *Compare the content overall and in detail.*
   **5**

4. How accurately does **Source E** illustrate Norman control over the church in England?
   *Use the source and recalled knowledge.*
   **6**

5. To what extent did the Normans succeed in expanding their power and influence in medieval Europe?
   *Use **Sources B**, **C** and **E** and recalled knowledge.*
   **8**

   **(30)**

*[END OF QUESTIONS ON SPECIAL TOPIC 1]*

## SPECIAL TOPIC 2: THE CRUSADES 1096–1204

**Study the sources below and then answer the questions which follow.**

**Source A:** is an account of Urban II's speech at Clermont, 1095, as recorded many years later by Robert the Monk.

Upon you, therefore, is the task of avenging these wrongs and of recovering this territory. God has conferred upon you remarkable glory in arms, great courage, bodily activity, and strength to humble the heads of those who resist you. Let the deeds of your ancestors encourage you and incite your minds to manly achievements: the greatness of King Charlemagne, and of his son Louis, and of your other monarchs, who have destroyed the kingdoms of the Turks and have extended the influence of the Church over lands previously possessed by the pagan.

Let the holy sepulchre of our Lord and Saviour, which is possessed by pagan nations, especially inspire you. The holy places are now treated with irreverence and contempt by unbelievers. Oh, most valiant soldiers, recall today the valour of your invincible ancestors.

**Source B:** is from *God's War*, by Christopher Tyerman (2006).

The shambles in the Balkans served as a prelude to disaster. Alexius advised Peter the Hermit against pressing forward immediately, and urged him to wait for the arrival of the rest of the forces being assembled. Reunited with Walter Sans-Avoir and reinforced with Italian troops, Peter was provided with a well-supplied base. There, the usual difficulty of countering the boredom in an army camp was exaggerated by regional rivalries and the nearby territory of the Seljuk Turks, whose capital in Asia Minor was at Nicea, only twenty five miles away. In September, French raiders penetrated to the walls of Nicea. Not to be undone, a contingent of Germans and Italians, under the leadership of Rainaldo, ranged further ahead, seizing a castle at Xerigordo near Nicea. There they were trapped and massacred by Seljuks from Nicea.

**Source C:** is written by Raymond d'Aguiliers, the Chaplain of Raymond of Toulouse. He recorded the events of the Battle of Antioch shortly after the fall of Jerusalem.

When Kerbogha, the leader of the Turks, heard that the Franks were advancing to battle, he was very anxious. "What is this?" he said. "Didn't you tell me the Franks were few and would not fight us?"

God sent down upon all His army a divine shower of rain, full of blessing. All those touched by this were filled with all grace and courage. This miracle also affected our horses no less. For whose horse failed until the fight was over, even though it had tasted nothing except the bark or leaves of trees for eight days?

When all our fighting men had left the city, five other lines of troops appeared among us. For our princes had drawn up only eight, and there were thirteen lines of troops outside the city. In the beginning of the march out to battle God so multiplied our army that we, who before seemed fewer than the enemy, were in the battle more numerous than they. And when our men had thus advanced and formed in line, the enemy turned in flight without giving us a chance to engage in battle.

**Source D:** is from *The Crusades through Arab Eyes* (1984) and tells the events of the Battle of Antioch from a Muslim perspective.

The Muslim army was decidedly not a united force, but a coalition of princes with conflicting interests. Everyone was aware of Kerbogha's desire to acquire more territory. Their real enemy was Kerbogha. If he emerged victorious from battle against the infidels, no city would escape his rule.

They were not alarmed at Christian attempts to retake Antioch; it was inconceivable that the Franks would create states of their own in Syria. The Franks had suffered famine during the past months, and Antioch's food reserves were practically exhausted.

If the Franks were ready to join the battle, Kerbogha did not want to frighten them, before they left the city, with an excessively massive attack, which would drive them back into the city. While the Franks continued their deployment, desertions began in the Muslim camp. There were accusations of treason and cowardice. Kerbogha asked for a truce, but the Franks charged without even responding to his offer. Realising his mounting isolation Kerbogha ordered a general retreat, which immediately degenerated into a rout.

**Source E:** is taken from the Itinerary of Richard I, based on eyewitness accounts. It was written in London sometime after the Third Crusade.

King Richard had not yet fully recovered from his illness. He was anxious to be doing things and he was eager especially to attend to the capture of Acre. He saw to it therefore that the city was attacked by his men so that, perhaps by divine grace, the deed might be accomplished in accord with his wishes. He had a latticework shed built (crude wooden shelter) and he ordered it to be taken to the trench outside the city walls. When his most experienced crossbowmen were in position, he had himself carried out on a silken stretcher, so that the Saracens might be awed by his presence and also so that he could encourage his men for the fight. His crossbow, with which he was experienced, was then put into action and many were killed by the missiles and spears which he fired. His miners also made an underground passage to the tower at which his siege engines were firing. The miners sought out the foundations of the tower and hacked out part of it. They filled up the hole with timbers which they set afire. Then the repeated hits of the stone missiles suddenly knocked the tower to bits.

*[END OF SOURCES FOR SPECIAL TOPIC 2]*

**SPECIAL TOPIC 2: THE CRUSADES 1096–1204**

**Answer *all* of the following questions.**

*Marks*

1. How useful is **Source A** as evidence of the motives of the Crusaders?
   *In reaching a conclusion you should refer to:*
   * *the origin and possible purpose of the source;*
   * *the content of the source;*
   * *recalled knowledge.*                                                                 5

2. How fully does **Source B** explain the failure of the People's Crusade?
   *Use the source and recalled knowledge.*                                                6

3. Compare the descriptions of the capture of Antioch given in **Source C** and **Source D**.
   *Compare the content overall and in detail.*                                            5

4. To what extent do **Sources A**, **B** and **E** describe the crusading ideal?
   *Use **Sources A**, **B** and **E** and recalled knowledge.*                             8

5. How fully does **Source E** describe the capture of Acre during the Third Crusade?
   *Use the source and recalled knowledge.*                                                6

(30)

*[END OF QUESTIONS ON SPECIAL TOPIC 2]*

## OPTION B: EARLY MODERN HISTORY

### SPECIAL TOPIC 3: SCOTLAND 1689–1715

**Study the sources below and then answer the questions which follow.**

**Source A:** from T. M. Devine, *The Scottish Nation* (1999).

This Parliament (1703) now seemed virtually outside the control of the Duke of Queensberry, the Queen's Commissioner, and his ministers and supporters. The resentment, which had been building up in earlier sessions, boiled over with a vengeance. First, the parliament refused to vote the financial supply. Second, an Act of Security was passed, in open defiance of Queensberry and the Court or governing party, stating that the Scots parliament had the right to decide on Queen Anne's successor and that England and Scotland could not have the same sovereign in the future unless the London Parliament granted the Scots "free communication of trade . . . and access to her colonies". Not surprisingly, the queen initially refused to give her assent, although she gave it reluctantly, in the following year. The ministry was then forced to accept the Act anent (concerning) Peace and War, which gave the Scots parliament the right to declare war and make peace if the two nations continued to share a sovereign after Anne's death. In the vain attempt to get financial supply in return for these concessions, the ministry allowed this to pass, despite the fact that its whole emphasis suggested a separate Scottish foreign policy.

**Source B:** from Lockhart of Carnwath, *Memoirs* (1714).

The ministers were concerned about the government of the Kirk, and roared against the wicked union from their pulpits, and sent addresses against it from several presbyteries and the Assembly. But no sooner did Parliament pass an act for the security of the Kirk than most of their zeal was cooled, and many of them changed their tune and preached in favour of it.

But the truth of the matter lies here: a sum of money was necessary to be distributed amongst the Scots. And this distribution of it amongst the proprietors of the Company of Scotland was the best way of bribing a nation . . . alas it had the desired effect.

**Source C:** from a pamphlet by Seton of Pitmedden, "*Scotland's great advantage by a Union with England*", (1706).

With Union, England secures an old and dangerous enemy to be her friend, and thereby ensures peace at home, and is more safe to conduct her policy abroad. Scotland will not be alarmed by the threatenings of a powerful and rich neighbour, not so easily put under the yoke of a foreign enemy. England gains a considerable addition of brave and courageous men to their fleet, armies and plantations, and Scotland is secured by their protection, and enriched by their labours. We send our produce and useful manufactured goods to them and have money and other things we need given to us. They have free access to all our seas and ports and are capable of all privileges of citizens. We are the same among them, can start colonies at a cheaper rate, and with more assurance than before.

**Source D:** from William Ferguson, *Scotland's Relations with England* (1977).

As it was, once the contents of the treaty had been leaked, nearly every sector of the Scottish nation found something objectionable in the proposed union. The Jacobites, rightly enough from their standpoint, saw it as a deadly blow to the hopes of the exiled Stewarts. The Episcopalians, most of whom favoured the Stewarts, were afraid that the union would secure Presbyterianism. The Presbyterians welcomed the protestant succession, but feared that, under the union, bishops would again be thrust upon the Church of Scotland. Strangely, the offer of free trade gained little enthusiasm in many of the royal burghs, incuding Glasgow.

**Source E:** from a letter from the Earl of Mar to the Earl of Oxford, 1711.

I am not yet tired of the union and still think it for the good of the whole island, and also that it is the only thing which can keep Scotland and England from bloodshed and disorder, so I am not sorry for any part I had in bringing it about. But, should the issue of the Peerage be dealt with unfairly and if our trade is not encouraged more than it has been so far, how is it possible that flesh and blood can bear it, and what Scotsman will not be tired of the union and do all he can to end it?

[END OF SOURCES FOR SPECIAL TOPIC 3]

### SPECIAL TOPIC 3: SCOTLAND 1689–1715

**Answer *all* of the following questions.**

*Marks*

1. How fully does **Source A** explain the growing tension between Scotland and England in the period up to 1705?
   *Use the source and recalled knowledge.*                                    **6**

2. How useful is **Source B** as evidence of the methods used to pass the Treaty of Union?
   *In reaching a conclusion you should refer to:*
   • *the origin and possible purpose of the source;*
   • *the content of the source;*
   • *recalled knowledge.*                                                      **5**

3. Compare the views expressed in **Source C** and **Source D** on the value of having a Treaty of Union.
   *Compare the content overall and in detail.*                                **5**

4. How far do **Sources A**, **B** and **C** explain why the Treaty of Union was passed?
   *Use **Sources A**, **B** and **C** and recalled knowledge.*                 **8**

5. How typical is **Source E** of attitudes towards the Treaty of Union in the period after 1707?
   *Use the source and recalled knowledge.*                                    **6**

(30)

[END OF QUESTIONS ON SPECIAL TOPIC 3]

## SPECIAL TOPIC 4: THE ATLANTIC SLAVE TRADE

**Study the sources below and then answer the questions which follow.**

**Source A:** from a speech by Lord Penrhyn during the Debate on the Slave Trade, House of Commons, 1788.

Mr. Speaker, let us have an enquiry. It will reveal that those concerned in the African Trade and the planters, both of whose characters have been blackened and their conduct grossly criticised, do not deserve this condemnation.

The abolition of the Slave Trade is unnecessary and impracticable. In considering the subject, I hope the House will not forget the trade, commerce, and navigation of this country.

There are no cruel practices! It is absurd to suppose that men, whose profit depends on the health and vigour of the African natives, would deliberately torment and distress them during the passage! We need a candid and careful investigation, and then you will find that all the idle stories of cruelty are complete lies.

I also have a petition from the merchants and traders of Liverpool. It states how much the country benefits from the Trade. My constituents have continued for many years to carry on the African Trade—they have had every reason to think it a legal trade. The Bill is an attack upon them, which is not justified by either fact or necessity.

**Source B:** From R. Anstey, *The Atlantic Slave Trade and British Abolition* (1975).

Wilberforce devoted much time to writing to his friends urging them to secure petitions from meetings in the counties; so did the London Abolition Committee. Clarkson helped to form the Newcastle and Nottingham abolition societies, whilst many other societies sprang up during the winter months. The association with radicalism came because the Manchester committee produced a petition with no less than 20,000 signatures. A number of abolitionists also renounced the use of sugar at this time. This appeal brought results in a way that had not been previously achieved by the abolitionists. Traditional methods, however, were not neglected: a sub-committee was set up to "wait upon" potential supporters in the House of Commons in order to strengthen the abolitionists' interest.

**Source C:** an account by Olaudah Equiano of his experience on board a slave ship on the Middle Passage in the 1750s after his capture in Nigeria.

When I was on board, I looked around the ship and I saw a multitude of black people of every description chained together, every one of their faces expressing dejection and sorrow. I was soon put down under the decks, and I became so sick with the stench that I was not able to eat. I wished for death to relieve me. When I refused to eat, two white men held me by the hands and laid me down and flogged me severely.

If I could have got over the nettings, I would have jumped over the side, but I could not. The white people acted in a savage manner. I had never seen among any people such instances of brutal cruelty. The closeness of the hold, the heat, and the number in the ship almost suffocated us. The air became unfit for breathing and brought on a sickness amongst the slaves, of which many died. This situation was aggravated by the chains, the shrieks of the women and the groans of the dying.

In this manner we continued to undergo more hardships than I can now relate.

**Source D:** from an eye-witness account by Alexander Falconbridge, a surgeon, of the experiences of slaves on board ship on the Middle Passage in 1788.

It often happens that slaves tumble over their companions in consequence of their being shackled together. In favourable weather they are fed upon deck, but in bad weather their food is given to them below deck. Their allowance of water is about half a pint each, at every meal. Upon the slaves refusing to take food, I have seen coals of fire put on a shovel and placed so near their lips as to burn them.

Most ships have air-hatches, but when the sea is rough and the rain heavy, these are shut. The exclusion of fresh air is intolerable. The Africans are more violently affected by sea-sickness than Europeans. It frequently ends in death, especially among the women. The ship's officers are sometimes guilty of such brutal excesses as disgrace human nature. The excruciating pain which the poor sufferers feel from being obliged to continue in so dreadful a situation is not to be conceived or described. The surgeon going between decks in the morning frequently finds several of the slaves dead.

**Source E:** from H. Thomas, *The Slave Trade: A History of the Atlantic Slave Trade 1440–1870* (1997).

By 1790 an alliance against abolition was forming at Westminster. This included articulate members of the royal family, of whom several were willing to speak and vote in Parliament; most of the admirals, active and retired; many landowners who feared any change; and, of course, the main commercial interests in London, such as people interested in cotton as well as sugar, for cotton was needed in the new industrial revolution even more than sugar. At that time, 70% of the cotton used in Britain came from the West Indies, and the income from the West Indian plantations was estimated by Prime Minister Pitt as £4,000,000 compared with £1,000,000 from the rest of the world.

*[END OF SOURCES FOR SPECIAL TOPIC 4]*

**SPECIAL TOPIC 4: THE ATLANTIC SLAVE TRADE**

**Answer *all* of the following questions.**

*Marks*

1. How fully does **Source A** illustrate the arguments used by British opponents of abolition?
   *Use the source and recalled knowledge.*                                                   **6**

2. How accurately does **Source B** identify the methods used by abolitionists?
   *Use the source and recalled knowledge.*                                                   **6**

3. How valuable is **Source C** as evidence of life for slaves on the Middle Passage?
   *In reaching a conclusion you should refer to:*
   • *the origin and possible purpose of the source;*
   • *the content of the source;*
   • *recalled knowledge.*                                                                      **5**

4. Compare the views expressed in **Source C** and **Source D** on the experiences of slaves in the Middle Passage.
   *Compare the content overall and in detail.*                                                **5**

5. To what extent do **Sources A**, **D** and **E** illustrate the range of opinions in the debate surrounding the slave trade?
   *Use **Sources A**, **D** and **E** and recalled knowledge.*                                 **8**
   **(30)**

*[END OF QUESTIONS ON SPECIAL TOPIC 4]*

## SPECIAL TOPIC 5: THE AMERICAN REVOLUTION

**Study the sources below and then answer the questions which follow.**

**Source A:** from a letter written by Benjamin Franklin during a visit to Britain.

Every man in England seems to consider himself to have sovereignty over America and seems to jostle himself into the throne with the King, and talks of "our subjects in the colonies." But America, an immense territory, with all the advantages of climate, soils, rivers, lakes, etc, must become a great country, populous and mighty; and will be able to shake off any shackles that may be imposed on her, and perhaps place them on the imposers. And yet there remains among the colonists so much respect and affection for Britain that, if cultivated prudently, with a kind tenderness, they might be easily governed for ages, without force or any considerable expense. But I do not see in London a sufficient quantity of the wisdom that is necessary to produce such a conduct, and I regret this.

**Source B:** from D. L. Ammerman, *The Tea Crisis and its Consequences* (2000).

It was possible to single out Boston and Massachusetts for punishment. Parliament adopted four specific Acts in direct response to the Boston Tea Party. The Boston Port Act closed the port of Boston. Declaring shipping to be unsafe in that area, Parliament forbade ships to enter or leave the port until compensation had been made for the tea. Even then, commerce would not be restored until the King determined that it was safe. The Massachusetts Government Act altered the basic structure of colonial government. It provided that the upper house, or Council, should henceforth be appointed by the King rather than selected by the governor from a list nominated by the lower house. The Justice Act was intended to protect British officials in their efforts to enforce the law. It provided that in capital cases government officials, or those working under their direction, be protected from vindictive local juries. The Quartering Act altered existing legislation in an effort to provide more effectively for British troops. It stipulated that when the colony offered quarters which were unacceptable, the governor could take over unoccupied public buildings for the use of the troops.

**Source C:** from a letter written by Lord George Germain in London to Lord Cornwallis in the colonies, June 4, 1781.

The promising rapidity of your movements through a country so thinly inhabited and so little cultivated is justly a matter of astonishment to all Europe as well as to the rebels in America. Although Washington's limited troops appear to make every possible exertion to oppose your progress and conduct their enterprises in Carolina with more spirit than they have shown in any other part of America, the outcome is certain. His Majesty has such confidence in your lordship's great military talents that he entertains no doubt of your fulfilling his utmost expectations of success in the course of your campaign.

**Source D:** from a letter from Benjamin Gilbert, an American soldier, to his father, September 19, 1781.

Military affairs in this area bear a more favourable aspect than they have for some time past. Count de Grasse has arrived with 28 ships and 5,200 French troops. General Washington has arrived with Count Rochambeau, and has 8,000 troops both French and American. The troops raised by Pennsylvania, Maryland and Virginia this summer are also with us in Carolina, so that makes our strength 16,000 regulars, plus artillery, cavalry and militia.

The French fleet has shut Lord Cornwallis into York River and he is fortifying himself in Yorktown where we expect to soon lay siege to him. If the French fleet continues to do this, and fate smiles on us, then we shall give as good an account of ourselves as we did against Burgoyne. Our spirits are kept high by the warmest expectations of capturing Cornwallis and his army.

**Source E:** from Gary B. Nash, *The Unknown American Revolution* (2005).

The year 1778 figured crucially for the American patriots. Benjamin Franklin's charm and genius in Paris plucked the American cause from near disaster. By engineering a treaty of commerce and unity with the French, announced in March 1778, the Americans soon celebrated the French declaration of war on Great Britain, and the arrival of French troops, a formidable French fleet, and great quantities of war material. American prospects brightened, at least momentarily.

Yet French intervention did not yet tip the balance. The French alliance kept the American nation in the war but could not enable them to win it. During the years from 1778 to 1781, when the fortunes of the quest for independence hung in the balance, the American Revolution had to be carried forward on multiple fronts.

*[END OF SOURCES FOR SPECIAL TOPIC 5]*

### SPECIAL TOPIC 5: THE AMERICAN REVOLUTION

**Answer *all* of the following questions.**

*Marks*

1. To what extent does **Source A** illustrate the issues which led to the growing colonial challenge to British authority by 1774?
   *Use the source and recalled knowledge.*      **6**

2. How fully does **Source B** identify the British policies which led to increased hostility from the colonists between 1774 and 1776?
   *Use the source and recalled knowledge.*      **6**

3. How useful is **Source C** as evidence of British progress in the war during 1781?
   *In reaching a conclusion you should refer to:*
   * *the origin and possible purpose of the source;*
   * *the content of the source;*
   * *recalled knowledge.*      **5**

4. Compare the views on the military situation in 1781, expressed in **Source C** and **Source D**.
   *Compare the content overall and in detail.*      **5**

5. How fully do **Sources C, D** and **E** explain the outcome of the War of Independence?
   *Use **Sources C, D** and **E** and recalled knowledge.*      **8**

   **(30)**

*[END OF QUESTIONS ON SPECIAL TOPIC 5]*

## OPTION C: LATER MODERN HISTORY

### SPECIAL TOPIC 6: PATTERNS OF MIGRATION: SCOTLAND 1830s–1930s

**Study the sources below and then answer the questions which follow.**

**Source A:** a photograph of a close in the High Street of Glasgow in the 1870s.

**Source B:** from *The Ayr Advertiser, 1849*.

Over most of Scotland a deplorable change is at present being made in the habits of the people . . . a change which is every day becoming more apparent, and which forms an increasing cause of alarm to those who have the interest of their native land at heart. Driven by the increasing poverty in their own country to emigrate to Scotland, by the enterprise of whose people railways are being formed and new and important sources of wealth opened up, the Irish, during the past ten years, have absolutely inundated this country. They have swallowed up our rapidly increasing Poor Rates, have directed charity away from its proper channels, and have filled our jails. By their great numbers they have lessened wages or totally deprived thousands of the working people of Scotland of that employment which legitimately belonged to them. Lastly, there can be no doubt that their contact with the Scotch has not been for the benefit morally or intellectually of the latter.

Let us redouble our efforts not to keep Scotland for the Scotch, for that is impossible; but to keep Scotland—Scotch! Scotch in religion, morality and intelligence.

**Source C:** from *"The Irish"*, History Today, Volume 35 (1985).

Certainly the Irish Catholic immigrants look like the outcasts of Victorian society, outcast from British business and enterprise as the poorest of the poor, from mainstream British politics as separatist Nationalists and Republicans, from the "Anglo-Saxon" race as "Celts", and as Catholics from the dominant forms of British Protestantism. The Irish were, thus, the outcasts of Victorian Britain, with an accumulated body of disadvantages possessed by no other group of immigrants. They were the largest unassimilated section of society, set apart and everywhere rejected and despised. In Glasgow, the Catholic Irish found jobs in mills and mines, although they were excluded from engineering, the shipyards which were dominated by the Orange Order, and skilled trades controlled by craft unions.

**Source D:** from the *Inverness Courier*, 30 May 1838.

After months of expectation and anxiety, the Government emigration agent for Australia, arrived at Fort William. The news of his arrival spread like wildfire, through every glen in the district. At a very early hour on the Monday, thousands of enterprising Highlanders, most with some capital and possessing marketable skills which were in demand in their newly adopted lands, were seen crowding around the Caledonian Hotel, anxious to leave the land of their ancestors and to go and possess the limitless quantity of land in Australia. While it is to be regretted that so many active men should feel it necessary to leave their own country, the Highlands will be considerably relieved of its surplus population. Further, the opportunities which exist for improving the lives of themselves and their families is too great an attraction for these men to ignore.

**Source E:** from *Adventurers and Exiles The Great Scottish Exodus* by Marjory Harper (2003).

For most emigrants, hope and adventure were far stronger sentiments than despair and resignation. Bitterness was rarely the sole reason for emigration; most often it was mixed with an element of ambition. At the very least, they anticipated an improvement on conditions and prospects at home, often for the sake of the next generation as much as for themselves. By no means were all emigrants destitute, disillusioned or driven out of their country of birth. Many had cash in their pockets as well as hope in their hearts. They were not reluctant refugees from a backward rural economy, but voluntary exiles from a vibrant, industrialising and increasingly urban society which offered good employment opportunities and a rising standard of living. Opponents of emigration frequently expressed concern at the loss of the best section of the Scottish population, those who were rich in skills and enterprise as well as capital.

*[END OF SOURCES FOR SPECIAL TOPIC 6]*

**SPECIAL TOPIC 6: PATTERNS OF MIGRATION: SCOTLAND 1830s–1930s**

**Answer *all* of the following questions.**

*Marks*

1. How useful is **Source A** as evidence of the kind of living conditions faced by Irish immigrants in Victorian Scotland?
   *In reaching a conclusion you should refer to:*
   * *the origin and possible purpose of the source;*
   * *the content of the source;*
   * *recalled knowledge.*                                                                 5

2. To what extent do the views expressed in **Source B** reflect the reaction of native Scots to Irish immigration?
   *Use the source and recalled knowledge.*                                               6

3. How fully do **Sources A**, **B** and **C** illustrate the problems faced by Irish immigrants to Scotland during the period 1830–1939?
   *Use **Sources A**, **B** and **C** and recalled knowledge.*                            8

4. Compare the views on Scottish emigration as expressed in **Source D** and **Source E**.
   *Compare the content overall and in detail.*                                           5

5. How fully does **Source E** explain the reasons for Scottish emigration?
   *Use the source and recalled knowledge.*                                               6

                                                                                         **(30)**

*[END OF QUESTIONS ON SPECIAL TOPIC 6]*

**SPECIAL TOPIC 7: APPEASEMENT AND THE ROAD TO WAR, TO 1939**

**Study the sources below and then answer the questions which follow.**

**Source A:** from Gordon Craig, *Germany 1866–1935* (1978).

As the troops moved in, Germany accused the French Government of having destroyed the Locarno Treaty by signing an agreement with the Soviet Union that was clearly directed against Germany, and stated that Germany's remilitarisation of the Rhineland was an act of self defence. Germany declared it was ready to negotiate with the French and Belgian governments for new demilitarised zones on both sides of their common border, to negotiate mutual guarantees against attacks from the air and to return to the League of Nations.

Germany's statement was enough not only to persuade a number of prominent politicians to come out openly in defence of the German action, but probably influenced the strong popular feeling that Germany had only done what other nations normally did, namely strengthened its borders against possible attack.

**Source B:** a cartoon by David Low in *The London Evening Standard,* 4 June, 1937.

Anthony Eden to Hitler and Mussolini
*"Excuse me, have you got a bit of string about you?"*

**Source C:** from the leading article in *The Dundee Courier and Advertiser*, 1 October, 1938.

*The Peacemaker.*

No returning hero ever had as enthusiastic a reception as Mr Chamberlain received in London yesterday. No longer is there any doubt that were it not for the right-mindedness and strong-heartedness of this one man, the most devastating of wars would be on us now. There is one consideration that outweighs all others and it is this—if we had gone to war to resist German claims in Czechoslovakia we should be fighting for a bad cause. Mr Chamberlain never lost grip of that essential point. The Czechoslovakian settlement, with the inclusion of three and a half million Germans in an alien republic, was one of the great blunders of the post war peace treaties.

If Hitler has won a victory it is because, for once, he has right on his side. It is that fact, always recognised by Mr Chamberlain, that helped him more than all his massive armed forces.

**Source D:** from a speech by Winston Churchill in the House of Commons, 5 October, 1938.

I will therefore begin by saying the most unpopular and most unwelcome thing. I will begin by saying what everybody would like to ignore or forget, namely that we have sustained a total and unmitigated defeat.

The utmost the Prime Minister has been able to secure by all his immense exertions, by all the great efforts and mobilisation which took place in this country, and by all the anguish and strain through which we have passed in this country, the utmost he has been able to gain for Czechoslovakia and in the matters which were in dispute has been that the German dictator, instead of snatching what he wants from the table, has been content to have it served to him course by course.

Our people should know that there has been gross neglect and deficiency in our defences. They should know that we have sustained a defeat without a war, the consequences of which will travel far with us along our road. They should know that we have passed an awful milestone in our history, when the whole balance of Europe has been deranged.

And do not suppose that this is the end. This is only the beginning of the reckoning.

**Source E:** from a speech by Winston Churchill to the New Commonwealth Society, November 25, 1936.

Europe is now approaching the most dangerous moment in history. The struggle which is now opening between rival forms of dictatorships and democracies threatens to disturb the internal peace of many countries. That alone would bring us into grave danger. Yet I feel that danger has been made worse by the development of the aeroplane. The aeroplane has put all countries and all parts of every country simultaneously at the mercy of a sudden blasting attack. Already helpless nations have accepted the bombing of open cities and the indiscriminate slaughter of civilians as the inevitable result of war.

It is this combination of new air power with the rise of dictatorships that has brought all countries into a danger unknown previously.

*[END OF SOURCES FOR SPECIAL TOPIC 7]*

### SPECIAL TOPIC 7: APPEASEMENT AND THE ROAD TO WAR, TO 1939

**Answer *all* of the following questions.**

*Marks*

1. How fully does **Source A** explain why remilitarisation of the Rhineland led to so little reaction from Britain and other European countries?
   *Use the source and recalled knowledge.*    **6**

2. How useful is **Source B** as evidence of the problems facing Britain caused by the Spanish Civil War?
   *In reaching a conclusion you should refer to:*
   * *the origin and possible purpose of the source;*
   * *the content of the source;*
   * *recalled knowledge.*    **5**

3. How much support was there, at the time, for the views expressed in **Source C**?
   *Use the source and recalled knowledge.*    **6**

4. Compare the views on the Munich Agreement expressed in **Source C** and **Source D**.
   *Compare the content overall and in detail.*    **5**

5. How fully do **Sources A**, **C** and **E** explain why Britain adopted a policy of appeasement towards Germany in the later 1930s?
   *Use **Sources A**, **C** and **E** and recalled knowledge.*    **8**

   **(30)**

*[END OF QUESTIONS ON SPECIAL TOPIC 7]*

**SPECIAL TOPIC 8: THE ORIGINS AND DEVELOPMENT OF THE COLD WAR 1945–1985**

**Study the sources below and then answer the questions which follow.**

**Source A:** from the memoirs of Nikita Khrushchev, *Khrushchev Remembers* (1971).

In 1956, a bloody struggle broke out in Budapest. Imre Nagy used intimidation to draw people into mutiny and war. He shoved prominent citizens in front of microphones and forced them to endorse his leadership and to denounce the Rakosi regime. Active members of the Party were being hunted down in the streets. People were being murdered, strung up from lamp posts, and hanged by their feet—there were all kinds of outrages. The NATO countries were adding fuel to the flames of the civil war in hopes that the revolutionary government would be overthrown, the gains of the revolution would be lost, and capitalism would be restored to Hungary.

**Source B:** from J. L. Gaddis, *The Cold War*, (2005).

Khrushchev intended his missile deployment in Cuba chiefly as an effort to spread revolution throughout Latin America. He and his advisers had been surprised when a Marxist–Leninist uprising seized power in Cuba on its own. But Castro's revolution was in danger. The Eisenhower administration had broken off diplomatic relations with Cuba and had begun plotting Castro's overthrow. Kennedy allowed these plans to go forward with the unsuccessful Bay of Pigs landing.

As Khrushchev saw it, the attempted invasion would surely be repeated, the next time with much greater force. "The fate of Cuba and the maintenance of Soviet prestige in that part of the world pre-occupied me", Khrushchev recalled. "We had to think up some way of confronting America with more than words. We had to establish an effective deterrent to American interference in the Caribbean. The logical answer was missiles."

**Source C:** from an "appeal" to the Czechoslovakian president from the Communist Party of the Soviet Union, 19 August 1968.

The governments of the Soviet Union, Poland, Hungary, the German Democratic Republic and Bulgaria received a request from a majority of the members of the Communist Party of Czechoslovakia and from many members of the Czech government to provide armed assistance to the Czechoslovak people to help them resist counter revolution and defend the gains of socialism in Czechoslovakia. Comrade Dubcek and several others are conducting themselves dishonestly and are supporting the activities of the reactionary forces. In accordance with this, the military units of our five countries will enter the territory of Czechoslovakia at midnight tonight. They will come to your country as faithful friends of the Czechoslovak people. They will not interfere in the internal affairs of your country and will leave the territory of Czechoslovakia whenever the president and government of Czechoslovakia deem this to be necessary.

**Source D:** from a statement by the Communist Party of Czechoslovakia, broadcast on 21 August, 1968.

On Tuesday, 20 August 1968, at approximately 11pm, the armies of the USSR, Poland, the German Democratic Republic, Hungary and Bulgaria crossed the borders of the Czechoslovak Socialist Republic. This occurred without the knowledge of the President of the Republic, the chairman of the National Assembly, the Prime Minister and the Communist Party First Secretary.

The Communist Party of Czechoslovakia Presidium calls on all citizens of the republic to remain calm and to refrain from putting up any resistance against the advancing troops, since it would now be impossible to defend our state borders.

Units of the Czechoslovak army and the People's Militia have received no orders to defend the republic. We believe that the border crossing not only breaks all principles governing relations between socialist states, but also violates the fundamental provisions of international law.

**Source E:** from William R. Keylor, *The Twentieth Century World*, (2001).

On May 10, 1955 the Kremlin formally proposed the destruction of nuclear stockpiles. In his speech to the UN General Assembly in 1959 Khrushchev advocated general and total disarmament within four years. But all of the proposals that came from the Soviet Union failed because of the question of verification: Washington insisted on onsite inspection to ensure compliance, while Moscow rejected the presence of foreign observers as an infringement of its national sovereignty. If superpower disarmament in an unstable world proved to be an impossible goal, the nuclear alarm sounded by the Cuban missile crisis prompted the two sides to concentrate on a more modest objective: limitations on the testing, deployment and proliferation of nuclear weapons in the future.

*[END OF SOURCES FOR SPECIAL TOPIC 8]*

### SPECIAL TOPIC 8: THE ORIGINS AND DEVELOPMENT OF THE COLD WAR 1945–1985

**Answer *all* of the following questions.**

*Marks*

1. How useful is **Source A** in explaining Soviet intervention in Hungary in 1956?
   *In reaching a conclusion you should refer to:*
   * *the origin and possible purpose of the source;*
   * *the content of the source;*
   * *recalled knowledge.*                                                   5

2. How fully does **Source B** explain the reasons for the USSR's plan to site nuclear weapons in Cuba?
   *Use the source and recalled knowledge.*                                 6

3. To what extent does **Source C** provide an adequate explanation for the invasion of Czechoslovakia by Warsaw Pact forces in 1968?
   *Use the source and recalled knowledge.*                                 6

4. Compare the views on military intervention in Czechoslovakia in 1968 expressed in **Source C** and **Source D**.
   *Compare the content overall and in detail.*                             5

5. How fully do **Sources A, B** and **E** explain the reasons for tension between the superpowers during the Cold War?
   *Use **Sources A**, **B** and **E** and recalled knowledge.*             8

   (30)

*[END OF QUESTIONS ON SPECIAL TOPIC 8]*

## SPECIAL TOPIC 9: IRELAND 1900–1985: A DIVIDED IDENTITY

**Study the sources below and then answer the questions which follow.**

**Source A:** is by Tom Barry who fought in the war and later became Chief of Staff for the IRA in the 1930s.

In June 1915, in my seventeenth year, I decided to see what this Great War was like. I cannot plead that I went on the advice of John Redmond or any other politician, that if we fought for the British we would secure Home Rule for Ireland, nor can I say I understood what Home Rule meant. I was not influenced by the lurid appeal to fight to save Belgium or small nations. I knew nothing about nations, large or small. I went to the war for no other reason than that I wanted to see what war was like, to get a gun, to see new countries and to feel a grown man.

**Source B:** George Bernard Shaw, speaking in 1916 about the Easter Rising.

My own view is that the men who were shot in cold blood, after their capture or surrender, were prisoners of war, and that it was therefore entirely incorrect to slaughter them.

Until British rule is superseded by a national parliament and Ireland voluntarily incorporated with the British Empire, an Irishman resorting to arms to achieve independence of his country, is doing only what Britons will do if it be their misfortune to be invaded and conquered by the Germans in the course of the present war. Further, such an Irishman is as much in order morally in accepting assistance from the Germans, in his struggle with Britain, as Britain is in accepting assistance of Russia in her struggle with Germany. It is absolutely impossible to slaughter a man in this position without making him a martyr and a hero. The shot Irishmen will now take their places beside earlier heroes; and nothing in Heaven or earth can prevent it. The military authorities and the British government must have known they were turning their prisoners into saints.

**Source C:** written by a Dublin woman at the time of the Easter Rising.

Of course this is not Ireland's rebellion—only a Sinn Fein rising. How often have I laughed and quarrelled over the very idea of an Irish Republic! It is so utterly un-Irish. Of course we want our own country free from foreign rule. But any one with sense must see that it must come by Britain's consent, not against Britain's will. The Sinn Fein leaders were such good men. They died like saints. Oh! The pity of it! And Ireland wanted them so much! They have brought great and terrible trouble on us and Ireland—but they meant to do the exact opposite. They have crushed us under a weight of sorrow and shame—but they meant the reverse. What wild madness came over them!

But, as sure as God's sun rises in the East, if Britain doesn't get things right—if there's not immediately conciliation, and love and mercy poured out on Ireland—all the Sinn Fein leaders will be seen as saints. You know how Ireland is always merciful to the dead.

**Source D:** from *Fighting for Dublin* by William Sheehan, 2007.

In the Irish imagination, the War of Independence is remembered primarily as a war of flying columns, a campaign in isolated hills and mountains. However, the insurgency in Dublin was a key focus of the British Army. Aeroplanes were used to disperse crowds near Mountjoy, distribute propaganda leaflets by air and provide armed protection to convoys and trains. Aerial reconnaissance was becoming important for the army, leading to the finding of arms dumps in the Wicklow Mountains, and for the monitoring of the IRA during the Truce. Armoured vehicles were routinely deployed in operations in Dublin, to provide greater protection for soldiers, conserve manpower and strengthen offensive operations, while searchlights were critical to the enforcement of the curfew. Stop and search methods were also improved by the British Army.

**Source E:** is from a speech by David Lloyd George in the House of Commons, 14 December 1921, commenting on the Anglo-Irish Treaty.

On the British side we have allegiance to the crown, partnership in the empire, security of our shores, security for Ulster. These are the provisions we have over and over again laid down, and they are here, signed in the document.

On the Irish side there is one supreme advantage—that the Irish people as a nation will be free in their own land to work out their own national destinies in their own way. These two nations, I believe, will be reconciled. Ireland, within her own boundaries, will be free to use her resources, direct her own forces—material, moral and spiritual—and guide her own destinies.

*[END OF SOURCES FOR SPECIAL TOPIC 9]*

### SPECIAL TOPIC 9: IRELAND 1900–1985: A DIVIDED IDENTITY

**Answer *all* of the following questions.**

*Marks*

1. How fully does **Source A** illustrate Irish attitudes to the First World War?
   *Use the source and recalled knowledge.*                                                                   6

2. Compare the views expressed in **Source B** and **Source C** on the Easter Rising.
   *Compare the content overall and in detail.*                                                               5

3. To what extent does **Source D** describe the conduct of both sides during the Anglo-Irish war?
   *Use the source and recalled knowledge.*                                                                   6

4. How useful is **Source E** as evidence of opinions on the Anglo-Irish Treaty?
   *In reaching a conclusion you should refer to:*
   * *the origin and possible purpose of the source;*
   * *the content of the source;*
   * *recalled knowledge.*                                                                                      5

5. How fully do **Sources B**, **D** and **E** explain the development of division and conflict in Ireland from 1912 onwards?
   *Use **Sources B**, **D** and **E** and recalled knowledge.*                                                8

                                                                                                              (30)

*[END OF QUESTIONS ON SPECIAL TOPIC 9]*

*[END OF QUESTION PAPER]*

[BLANK PAGE]

[BLANK PAGE]

# X044/301

NATIONAL
QUALIFICATIONS
2010

WEDNESDAY, 26 MAY
9.00 AM – 10.20 AM

HISTORY
HIGHER
Paper 1

Answer questions on **one** Option only.

Take particular care to show clearly the Option chosen.  On the **front** of the answer book, **in the top right-hand corner**, write A or B or C.

Within the Option chosen, answer **two** questions, one from Historical Study:  Scottish and British and one from Historical Study:  European and World.

All questions are worth 20 marks.

Marks may be deducted for bad spelling and bad punctuation, and for writing that is difficult to read.

[BLANK PAGE]

## OPTION A:  MEDIEVAL HISTORY

**Answer TWO questions, one from Historical Study:  Scottish and British
and one from Historical Study:  European and World**

### Historical Study:  Scottish and British

**Medieval Society**

1.  How significant was the role of knights in medieval society?

2.  How important was the contribution of the Church in twelfth century Scotland and England?

3.  "Towns and burghs grew rapidly in the twelfth and thirteenth centuries primarily because of the development of international trade."  How accurate is this statement?

4.  To what extent did David I create a 'Norman' Scotland?

5.  How successful were Henry II's attempts to reform law and order in twelfth century England?

### Historical Study:  European and World

**EITHER**

**Nation and King**

6.  "Financial difficulties were the main reason for the growth of baronial opposition during the reign of King John."  How valid is this view?

7.  How important was the development of central government in France in expanding royal power during the reign of Philip II?

8.  How important were the Scottish Wars of Independence in helping create a sense of Scottish identity?

9.  How significant was the contribution of Robert Bruce in helping Scotland to victory in the Scottish Wars of Independence?

**OR**

**Crisis of Authority**

10.  "The most significant outcome of the Hundred Years War was its economic impact on England and France."  How valid is this view?

11.  How important were events such as the Peasants' Revolt and the Jacquerie in bringing about the end of serfdom?

12.  To what extent can it be argued that the Black Death had a devastating effect on European Society?

13.  "The Conciliar Movement, despite some early success, was unable to fully solve the problems facing the Church in the fifteenth century."  How accurate is this statement?

## OPTION B:  EARLY MODERN HISTORY

**Answer TWO questions, one from Historical Study:  Scottish and British and one from Historical Study:  European and World**

### Historical Study:  Scottish and British

**EITHER**

### Scotland in the Age of the Reformation 1542–1603

1. To what extent were developments in Scotland between 1542 and 1548 influenced by the conflicting interests of England and France?

2. How important was English intervention in the success of the Reformation in Scotland?

3. To what extent were the difficulties faced by Mary Queen of Scots in ruling Scotland the result of religious divisions?

4. "The main problems facing James VI up to 1603 were issues of law and order."  How accurate is this statement?

5. How significant was the desire for the English throne in influencing the policies followed by James VI up to 1603?

**OR**

### Scotland and England in the Century of Revolutions 1603–1702

6. How important were disputes with Parliament in causing challenges to the authority of James VI and I after 1603?

7. To what extent were financial issues the main cause of the Civil War?

8. How far was religious freedom the main aim of the Covenanting movement?

9. To what extent was dependence on the military the reason for Cromwell's failure to establish successful government?

10. "Nothing changed apart from the monarch."  How valid is this view of the Revolution Settlement?

## Historical Study:  European and World

**EITHER**

### Royal Authority in 17th and 18th Century Europe

11.  How important were the Councils in maintaining the authority of Louis XIV?

12.  To what extent did Louis XIV's foreign policy have a damaging effect on France?

13.  "More concerned with increasing the power of the Prussian state, rather than improving the lives of his subjects."  How valid is this view of the reign of Frederick II?

14.  How far did Joseph II succeed in his aims of reforming the Austrian Empire?

**OR**

### The French Revolution:  The Emergence of the Citizen State

15.  "The failure to reform the financial system was the most serious threat to the Ancien Regime."  How valid is this statement?

16.  How important was the revolt of the nobles in 1787 as a cause of the revolution of 1789?

17.  "Constitutional monarchy in France was short-lived and doomed to fail."  How accurate is this view of French Government between 1789 and 1792?

18.  To what extent did the effects of war make it difficult to establish stable government in France between 1793 and 1799?

**[Turn over**

## OPTION C: LATER MODERN HISTORY

**Answer TWO questions, one from Historical Study: Scottish and British
and one from Historical Study: European and World**

**Historical Study: Scottish and British**

**Britain 1850s–1979**

1. To what extent did Britain make progress towards democracy between 1850 and 1918?

2. How successfully did the Liberal Reforms, of 1906–1914, deal with the problem of poverty in Britain in the early 1900s?

3. "The steady pressure by the moderate Suffragists was the most important reason for the achievement of votes for women by 1918." How accurate is this view?

4. How far did the post-war Labour Government meet the welfare needs of the British people between 1945 and 1951?

5. **Either**

   (a) "Urbanisation was the main factor in causing changes to leisure activities, religion and education in Scotland between 1880 and 1939." How accurate is this statement?

   **Or**

   (b) How far did changes in the Scottish economy influence the level of support for the Scottish National Party up to 1979?

## Historical Study:  European and World

**EITHER**

**The Growth of Nationalism**

*Germany*

6. To what extent were religious divisions in Germany the main obstacle to unification between 1815 and 1850?

7. How far was Bismarck's success in unifying Germany between 1862 and 1871 due mainly to mistakes made by others?

8. How successful was the new German state in dealing with internal political problems between 1871 and 1914?

9. "Propaganda rather than solid achievement allowed the Nazis to maintain their authority between 1933 and 1939."  How accurate is this view?

*Italy*

10. To what extent was the attitude of the papacy the main obstacle to Italian unification between 1815 and 1850?

11. "Cavour's diplomacy was the key to Italian unification."  How accurate is this view?

12. To what extent did the new Italian state win popular support in Italy during the period 1871 to 1914?

13. "Propaganda rather than solid achievement allowed the Fascists to maintain their authority between 1922 and 1939."  How accurate is this view?

**[Turn over for The Large Scale State on *Page eight***

**OR**

**The Large Scale State**

*The USA*

14. "The economic boom of the 1920s was largely due to the policies of the Republican administration." How valid is this statement?

15. How far was the Ku Klux Klan to blame for the problems black Americans faced in the 1920s and 1930s?

16. How far was the growth of the Civil Rights movement in the 1950s and 1960s due to the emergence of effective black leaders?

17. "Civil Rights improved for black Americans by 1968 mainly due to the actions of the federal government." How accurate is this view?

*Russia*

18. How significant was the role of the Okhrana in maintaining the authority of the Tsarist state in the years before 1905?

19. To what extent was the 1905 Revolution caused by the incompetence of the Tsar?

20. "The popularity of Bolshevik policies was the main reason for their success in seizing power in October 1917." How valid is this view?

21. To what extent were divisions among the Whites the reason for Bolshevik victory in the Civil War?

*[END OF QUESTION PAPER]*

# X044/302

NATIONAL
QUALIFICATIONS
2010

WEDNESDAY, 26 MAY
10.40 AM – 12.05 PM

HISTORY
HIGHER
Paper 2

Answer questions on only **one** Special Topic.

Take particular care to show clearly the Special Topic chosen. On the **front** of the answer book, **in the top right-hand corner**, write the number of the Special Topic.

You are expected to use background knowledge appropriately in answering source-based questions.

Marks may be deducted for bad spelling and punctuation, and for writing that is difficult to read.

Some sources have been adapted or translated.

[BLANK PAGE]

## OPTION A:  MEDIEVAL HISTORY

### SPECIAL TOPIC 1:  NORMAN CONQUEST AND EXPANSION 1050–1153

**Study the sources below and then answer the questions which follow.**

**Source A:** The movements of Tostig, from the *Ecclesiastical History of Orderic Vitalis*, Book III written between 1109 and 1124.

Banished from home, Tostig sought refuge in Flanders and gave his wife Judith into the charge of his father-in-law Baldwin, Count of Flanders.  He himself hurried to Normandy, boldly rebuked Duke William for allowing his perjured vassal to rule, and swore that he would faithfully secure the throne for him if he would cross to England with a Norman army.

Meanwhile, Tostig gained the Duke's permission to return to England, and promised faithfully that he and all his friends would give him every assistance.

**Source B:** from *Anglo-Norman England* by Marjorie Chibnall (1987).

For the first five years, the danger of rebellion backed by external enemies was never absent.  In 1068 troubles began in the west, when the men of Exeter arose.

Once William had captured the city, he began building a castle and established Baldwin, Richard fitz Gilbert's brother, as castellan.  He himself advanced further into Cornwall.

It was important for the King to control the shores of the Bristol Channel as firmly as possible, because of the danger of invasion from Ireland where some English exiles had taken refuge.

**Source C:** from the Charter by David I, c. 1128, founding the Burgh of Canongate.

And I grant to them a right to build for safety and residence a burgh between the same church (Holyrood) and my burgh (Edinburgh) and I grant that their burgesses shall have rights enjoyed in common of selling their saleable goods and of buying in my market freely and without challenge and without paying custom, just like my own burgesses; and I forbid anyone to seize in their burgh, bread or ale or cloth or any other saleable commodity by force or contrary to the will of the burgesses.

**Source D:** from *The Conquest of England*, E. Linklater (1966).

There is little record of how the peasantry fared under Norman occupation.  It is safe to assume that they suffered less than thanes and their class, for the thanes could be replaced by suitably enfeoffed Norman knights, but there were no substitutes for tillers of the soil.

Laws were strict and therefore respected, and behind the law there was a powerful church, and a responsible aristocracy.

Much has been made of the savage enforcement of the laws devised for the protection of game.  There is no disputing the fact that William, in his creation of the New Forest, drove out the inhabitants of many villages for the better protection of deer.  The Forest laws, though not of foreign origin, acquired a foreign look by the extension and the rigour of their application.

**Source E:** from the *Anglo-Saxon Chronicle*.

Amongst other things, the good order that William established is not to be forgotten. It was such that any man might travel over the kingdom with a bosom full of gold unmolested, and no man dare kill another, however great the injury he has received from him.

Truly, there was much trouble in those times, and very great distress. William caused castles to be built and oppressed the poor. The king was also of great sternness, and he took from his subjects many marks of gold.

He also made large forests for the deer, and enacted laws so that whoever killed a deer should also be blinded. As he forbade killing the deer, so also the boars—he loved the tall stags as if he were their father. He also commanded concerning the hares, that they should go free. The rich complained, and the poor grew angry, but he was so sturdy that he took no notice of them.

*[END OF SOURCES FOR SPECIAL TOPIC 1]*

**SPECIAL TOPIC 1: NORMAN CONQUEST AND EXPANSION 1050–1153**

**Answer *all* of the following questions.**

*Marks*

1. How fully does **Source A** explain William's actions in overthrowing Harold in 1066?
   *Use the source and recalled knowledge.* **6**

2. How far does **Source B** demonstrate William's ability to retain control in England immediately after the Conquest?
   *Use the source and recalled knowledge.* **6**

3. How useful is **Source C** as evidence of the development of feudalism in Scotland under David I?
   *In reaching a conclusion you should refer to:*
   • *the origin and possible purpose of the source;*
   • *the content of the source;*
   • *recalled knowledge.* **5**

4. To what extent do **Source D** and **Source E** agree about the lives of English peasants after the Conquest?
   *Compare the content overall and in detail.* **5**

5. How successfully did the Normans establish their authority over England?
   *Use **Sources B**, **D** and **E** and recalled knowledge.* **8**

**(30)**

*[END OF QUESTIONS ON SPECIAL TOPIC 1]*

## SPECIAL TOPIC 2: THE CRUSADES 1096–1204

**Study the sources below and then answer the questions which follow.**

**Source A:** from the *Alexiad* by Anna Commena, written in 1140.

When Bohemond, this evil man, had left his country in which he possessed no wealth at all under the pretext of adoring at the Lord's Sepulchre, but in reality endeavouring to acquire for himself a kingdom, he found himself in need of much money, especially, if he was to seize the Roman power. He followed the advice of his father and was leaving no stone unturned.

The Emperor, who understood fully Bohemond's wicked intention, skilfully managed to remove anything that might help further his ambitions. The Emperor knew that Bohemond was seeking a home for himself in the East by using great scheming, but he did not obtain it. The Emperor warned Raymond of Toulouse to keep a close watch against the malice of Bohemond, so that Raymond could immediately check him if he was to break his agreement with the Emperor and to strive in every way to destroy Bohemond's schemes. Raymond replied: "Since Bohemond has inherited perjury and deceit, it would be very surprising if he should be faithful to those promises which he has made under oath".

**Source B:** from *God's War, A New History of the Crusades* by Christopher Tyerman (2006).

Bohemond of Taranto is the most controversial leader of the First Crusade. Of all the major surviving commanders, he alone failed to join the march to Jerusalem in 1099, more concerned with securing his hold over Antioch. Admired for his generalship, his religious credentials have been discredited in the light of his attempts to carve out for himself a kingdom in the Balkans at the expense of the Byzantine Empire. The traditional view sees his motives as a desire for material gain, in contrast to the supposedly more pious and elevated goals of his colleagues. This is hard to say with any degree of accuracy; the psychologies of the crusade's leaders cannot be reconstructed. Each can be shown to have as much greed or as little piety as the other. Raymond of Toulouse, whose religious sincerity has been widely accepted, proved to be both scheming and childish in his quest for an eastern principality. Bohemond was not alone in his desire to achieve status, land and wealth. With Baldwin he undertook a dangerous journey to fulfil his pilgrimage to Jerusalem at Christmas 1099, a gesture that cannot be assured to have been purely for reasons of image or politics.

**Source C:** from the *Chronicle of Rigord*, a French monk written between 1180 and 1196. It refers to the growing dispute between Philip Augustus and Richard I.

King Philip wanted to start the assault on Acre first thing the next day. But the king of England would not permit his men to leave and forbade the Pisans, with whom he had an agreement, to assault, and so the assault failed. After consultation with both sides, spokesmen were chosen, wise and honest men by whose judgement and counsel the whole army was to be governed. The two kings promised and swore by God, that they would do whatever the two spokesmen said. The two arbiters said that the king of England should send his men into the assault, and have mangonels and other engines raised up, because the king of the Franks did all these things. He refused this, so king Philip released his own men from the oath which he had made about the government of the army.

What food and supplies that were found in Acre the Christians divided among themselves. But the kings had all the captives for themselves and divided them equally. The king of France however handed over half to the duke of Burgundy, together with much gold and silver and food. To the same duke he also entrusted his armies. For the king of France was actually sick of a very grievous illness, and he looked upon the king of England with much suspicion because Richard was sending envoys to Saladin and giving and receiving gifts from the Muslims.

**Source D:** an illumination from the *Histoire de Outremer* from the late thirteenth century.  It shows the massacre of Acre.

**Source E:** from *Medieval Europe* by H. G. Koenigsberger, (1987).

For a generation after the middle of the twelfth century, Christian Europe was too occupied with its own problems to think of crusades.  Its emperors and popes, its princes and knights chose to fight each other rather than the infidel.

The fall of Jerusalem rekindled crusading fervour in the west.  Once again, pope and preachers called for a united effort of Latin Christendom.  This time the organisation of the crusade was a great deal more professional than it had ever been before.  Rulers imposed special taxes, the Saladin tithe.  But the basic problems had not changed:  the need for a long and exhausting overland march through the Balkans or expensive and inadequate transport by sea; the not unjustified suspicion of Byzantium; the high numbers of dead among the crusaders; most of all the inevitable quarrels of the leaders, both with themselves and the Frankish princes of Outremer.

*[END OF SOURCES FOR SPECIAL TOPIC 2]*

**SPECIAL TOPIC 2:  THE CRUSADES 1096–1204**

**Answer *all* of the following questions.**

*Marks*

1.  How fully does **Source A** illustrate the attitudes of the leaders of the First Crusade?
    *Use the source and recalled knowledge.*

    **6**

2.  Compare the views of Bohemond of Taranto expressed in **Source A** and **Source B**.
    *Compare the content overall and in detail.*

    **5**

3.  How fully does **Source C** explain the reasons for Philip of France's decision to return home after the capture of Acre?
    *Use the source and recalled knowledge.*

    **6**

4.  How useful is **Source D** as evidence of the Massacre of Acre during the Third Crusade?
    *In reaching a conclusion you should refer to:*
    * *the origin and possible purpose of the source;*
    * *the content of the source;*
    * *recalled knowledge.*

    **5**

5.  To what extent was religion the main factor motivating the Crusades?
    *Use **Sources A**, **C** and **E** and recalled knowledge.*

    **8**

    **(30)**

*[END OF QUESTIONS ON SPECIAL TOPIC 2]*

## OPTION B: EARLY MODERN HISTORY

### SPECIAL TOPIC 3: SCOTLAND 1689–1715

**Study the sources below and then answer the questions which follow.**

**Source A:** from a pamphlet addressed to the Scottish Parliament, written by two Edinburgh publishers, 1700.

We beg you to consider, how our sovereignty and freedom is violated. Our laws have been trampled upon and our trade interrupted; our brothers have been starved and enslaved; our colony deserted, and our ships burnt and lost. We ask you to consider how the English ought to have let us have provisions, and ought to have protected us with their ships, since we share one sovereign. They allowed us to die for want of food and would not let us use our own naval vessels.

**Source B:** from A. Macinnes, *Union and Empire*, (2007).

While Queensberry, as the queen's commissioner, was prepared to accept the Act anent Peace and War, he did not give consent to the Act of Security until he received fresh instructions from London. Anne emphatically rejected what she considered unreasonable demands by the Scots. Before formal withholding of consent was received, Marchmont tried to get the Hanoverian succession accepted. But an Abjuration Act disowning the exiled royal family was thrown out.

The Darien scheme, the manoeuvring of Scotland into the war of the Spanish Succession and, indeed, the failed negotiations of early 1703 had taken their political toll. Patriotism now wore a particularly Scottish guise, with Fletcher of Saltoun speaking against the influence of the deceitful English ministry. Once the Estates were notified that royal consent was withheld, they declined to vote supply for the Scottish forces in the standing army.

**Source C:** from a petition by the Royal Burgh of Stirling, 1706.

We judge that going into this Treaty will bring an insupportable burden of taxation upon this land, which all the grants of freedom of trade will never counterbalance. We remain still under the control of the English in the Parliament of Britain, who may at their pleasure discourage the most important branches of our trade, if it was considered to interfere with theirs.

The Treaty will ruin our industries. It will threaten our religion, church government by law established, our Claim of Right, Laws, Liberties and all that's valuable.

One of the most ancient nations so long and so gloriously defended by our worthy patriots will be ended. Our parliament will be extinguished.

**Source D:** from Sir John Clerk of Penicuik, *Memoirs*, 1730.

The union of the two kingdoms was thought of as the best way to preserve the honour and liberty of Scotland and so the peace of the whole island. If the parliaments were united, the succession would pass to the same person. This was the principle motive both in Scotland and in England for bringing about the union. There were indeed other reasons which had greater influence on many in Scotland, such as the prohibition of the black cattle trade with England, a general mismanagement and decline in trade, a shortage of money to engage in other projects and the inability to enlarge our trade and improve our industry. Also, there was the suspicion that England would never allow us to grow rich and powerful as a separate state.

**Source E:** from C. Whatley, *The Scots and the Union*, 2007.

Without the Equivalent the Scots would never have any financial satisfaction for Darien. Given the blow that the loss of Darien had been to Scottish commercial ambitions and the subsequent economic difficulties, the promised injection of Equivalent funds into the Scottish economy would have been welcomed.

Although there were still reservations about the extent of Scottish representation in the new British parliament, in most other matters the treaty seemed to satisfy the Scottish Commissioners. Built into the incorporating union were elements of federalism: Scots Law and the retention of the main civil and criminal courts in Scotland for all time. There would be an independent Scottish privy council, although the new Parliament would have the right to amend it, or find an alternative. The rights and privileges of the Royal Burghs were to be left untouched.

*[END OF SOURCES FOR SPECIAL TOPIC 3]*

### SPECIAL TOPIC 3: SCOTLAND 1689–1715

**Answer *all* of the following questions.**

*Marks*

1. How useful is **Source A** as evidence of feelings in Scotland at the failure of the Darien scheme?
   *In reaching a conclusion you should refer to:*
   - *the origin and possible purpose of the source;*
   - *the content of the source;*
   - *recalled knowledge.*                                                                                 5

2. How fully does **Source B** describe the issues causing tension between Scotland and England in the period 1701–1705?
   *Use the source and recalled knowledge.*                                                              6

3. How typical is **Source C** of the views of the Scottish people at this time?
   *Use the source and recalled knowledge.*                                                              6

4. Compare the views on the benefits of Union as expressed in **Source C** and **Source D**.
   *Compare the content overall and in detail.*                                                          5

5. How adequately do **Sources B**, **D** and **E** illustrate the issues that led to the acceptance of the Treaty of Union?
   *Use **Sources B**, **D** and **E** and recalled knowledge.*                                          8

                                                                                                       **(30)**

*[END OF QUESTIONS ON SPECIAL TOPIC 3]*

## SPECIAL TOPIC 4: THE ATLANTIC SLAVE TRADE

**Study the sources below and then answer the questions which follow.**

**Source A:** from a speech made by Colonel Tarleton M.P., on the 18th April 1791.

Abolition would instantly annihilate a trade that annually employs upwards of 5500 sailors, upwards of 160 ships, and exports which amount to £700 000 annually.

It has been found out by experience that the natives of Europe could not work in the heat of the West Indies. Therefore the planter must be able to use Africans for the cultivation of his property. Anyone who knows the West Indies can estimate the value of slaves at £7 million. If therefore this commerce to Africa and the West Indies was stopped, it is not only the planter who would lose out. A yearly loss of £6 million would arise to the manufacturers, shipbuilders and a great many working people who would become unemployed.

**Source B:** a selection of artefacts: from left to right—Medallion produced by Wedgwood c. 1790, with the inscription: "Am I not a man and a brother"—Sugar Bowl, c. 1800 with the inscription "East India Sugar not made by Slaves" and a Patch Box in which ladies kept their artificial beauty spots, c. 1790.

**Source C:** from an account of a speech made by William Wilberforce, in the House of Commons, 1789.

Let any one imagine to himself 600 or 700 of these wretches chained two by two, surrounded with every object that is nauseous and disgusting, diseased and struggling under every kind of wretchedness! How can we bear to think of such a scene as this?

The song and the dance, says Mr Norris, are promoted. It had been more fair, perhaps, if he had explained that word promoted. The truth is, that for the sake of exercise, these miserable wretches, loaded with chains, oppressed with disease and wretchedness, are forced to dance by the terror of the lash, and sometimes by the actual use of it. Such, then is the meaning of the word promoted; and it may be observed too, with respect to food, that an instrument is sometimes carried out, in order to force them to eat which is the same sort of proof how much they enjoy themselves in that instance also.

Death, at least, is a sure ground of evidence, and the proportion of deaths will not only confirm but, if possible, will even aggravate our suspicion of their misery on the voyage. It will be found that, in an average of all the ships of which evidence has been given at the Privy Council, not less than 12·5 percent perish in the passage. Besides these, the Jamaica report tells you, not less than 4·5 per cent die on shore before the day of sale, which is only a week or two from the time of landing.

**Source D:** from R. Anstey, *The Atlantic Slave Trade and British Abolition* (1975).

If slave mutinies were most common when the slaver was still on the coast, they also happened during the middle passage. To prevent them, the men slaves were usually kept shackled in pairs while below, or by a loose chain when on deck, but were sometimes released during the crossing if it were felt that they had become reconciled to their fate. The women and boys were not normally shackled.

Two meals a day were normal but occasionally three were given. If two, one would be yams or rice, while the other would consist of foods like barley, corn and biscuit and, rarely, meat, the whole thing being boiled up into "a warm mess".

Exercise was regarded as necessary and this was done by "dancing". Defenders of the trade tried to make out that this was done with good cheer on deck; in fact, the dance consisted of jumping up and down rhythmically to the extent that loose shackles permitted, encouraged by the cat-o'-nine-tails.

**Source E:** from James Walvin, *The Cause of a Nation*, BBC history magazine (2007).

Oddly, the abolitionist cause was given an unexpected boost by the rise of Napoleon and his efforts to restore French slavery. It was the perfect opportunity for abolitionists to assert British superiority over the French.

The Foreign Slave Trade Act of 1806 had the effect of abolishing two thirds of Britain's slave trade. Traders and planters were caught completely unawares. The Lords spoke strongly against it but the old political stumbling block, William Pitt, was dead and was replaced by Lord Grenville, who was both abolitionist and able to influence events in the Lords.

To cap it all, the general election of 1806 saw large numbers of abolitionist MPs returned to Westminster.

[*END OF SOURCES FOR SPECIAL TOPIC 4*]

**SPECIAL TOPIC 4: THE ATLANTIC SLAVE TRADE**

**Answer *all* of the following questions.**

*Marks*

1.  To what extent are the arguments in **Source A** typical of those who supported the slave trade?
    *Use the source and recalled knowledge.*

    **6**

2.  How useful is **Source B** as evidence of the methods used by the Abolitionists?
    *In reaching a conclusion you should refer to:*
    *   *the origin and possible purpose of the source;*
    *   *the content of the source;*
    *   *recalled knowledge.*

    **5**

3.  To what extent does **Source C** illustrate the arguments of those who supported abolition of the slave trade?
    *Use the source and recalled knowledge.*

    **6**

4.  To what extent do **Source C** and **Source D** agree about the conditions on the middle passage?
    *Compare the content overall and in detail.*

    **5**

5.  How fully do **Sources B**, **C** and **E** identify why the abolition movement succeeded in ending the Slave Trade?
    *Use **Sources B**, **C** and **E** and recalled knowledge.*

    **8**

    **(30)**

[*END OF QUESTIONS ON SPECIAL TOPIC 4*]

## SPECIAL TOPIC 5: THE AMERICAN REVOLUTION

**Study the sources below and then answer the questions which follow.**

**Source A:** from the *Declaration of Rights and Grievances* approved by the delegates in the First Continental Congress of 1774.

The inhabitants of the English Colonies in North America have the following rights:

1. They are entitled to life, liberty and property, and they have never given any sovereign power the right to dispose of these without their consent.

2. They are entitled to participate in their own legislative council, which is the foundation of English liberty. As the colonists are not represented in the British Parliament, they should be entitled to a free and exclusive power of legislation, taxation and internal government in the colonies where their right of representation can be preserved.

3. The exercise of legislative power in the colonies by those appointed by the Crown is unconstitutional, dangerous and destructive to the freedom of American legislation.

**Source B:** from the pamphlet *Common Sense* by Thomas Paine, January 1776.

Arms as a last resort must decide the contest. The continent would accept any appeal by the king. Yet I challenge the warmest supporter of reconciliation to show a single advantage that this continent can obtain by being connected with Great Britain. Not a single advantage is being derived currently, but the injuries and disadvantages you are forced to sustain by that connection are numerous. Your duty to yourselves makes it vital that you do renounce the association with Britain.

It is unreasonable to suppose that France and Spain will give you any kind of assistance if you strengthen the connection between Britain and America. Under your present status as British subjects, you can neither be received nor heard abroad. The position of all foreign courts is against you, and will be so, until with independence you take your place amongst other nations.

**Source C:** from C. Bonwick, *The American Revolution* (1991).

The drift towards independence continually gathered pace. Most conventions in the colonies continued to instruct their delegates to seek reconciliation, but British policy made the prospect less and less probable. George III and his government had already decided that forcing the colonies into submission was the only alternative to permitting them to break their link with Britain. Throughout 1775, British reinforcements were gathered and 17,000 German mercenaries were hired. No notice was taken of the colonists' Olive Branch Petition. Instead, on 23 August, the king issued a proclamation declaring the colonies to be in rebellion.

By May 1776 the gathering momentum was virtually unstoppable. Most delegates realised that a decision was vital for practical reasons. Congress was increasingly aware that obtaining loans, arms and military supplies through making foreign agreements would be easier if it could secure recognition as an independent sovereign power.

**Source D:** from D. O. Winterbottom, *The American Revolution* (1972).

Cornwallis did not realise the importance of sea-power either to his own forces or to the enemy. If the British ever had any chance of crushing the colonists it was in the early years of the war while the conflict remained a private affair between Britain and the colonies. With Britain's failure to put down rebellion and the disaster at Saratoga, France entered the war and changed the whole complexion of the contest. Britain was required not only to fight the American colonies but to defend her empire in India and the West Indies as well as the shores of England herself. Britain had no allies, and was now fighting against the combined forces of the American colonies and France. The task was too great for her resources. Britain lost command of the sea. French intervention was decisive: it made British defeat only a matter of time.

**Source E:** from notes by Nicholas Cresswell, a British traveller, in America during 1777.

Washington is certainly a most surprising man, one of nature's geniuses. It is astonishing that he keeps General Howe at bay, even forces him to retreat. He has been a successful leader. From everything I have learned of him, I believe him to be a worthy, honest man, guilty of no bad habits, except perhaps being naturally ambitious. As an officer he is popular, idolised in the South. Some of the people look up to him as the saviour of their country and have confidence in everything he does. Congress look upon him as a necessary tool to achieve their purpose. He certainly deserves merit as a general.

*[END OF SOURCES FOR SPECIAL TOPIC 5]*

### SPECIAL TOPIC 5: THE AMERICAN REVOLUTION

**Answer *all* of the following questions.**

*Marks*

1. How accurately does **Source A** illustrate the issues surrounding the colonial challenge to British authority between 1760 and 1774?
   *Use the source and recalled knowledge.*    **6**

2. To what extent do **Sources B** and **C** agree about the situation faced by the colonists before the Declaration of Independence?
   *Compare the content overall and in detail.*    **5**

3. How fully does **Source D** explain the impact of French intervention in the war?
   *Use the source and recalled knowledge.*    **6**

4. How useful is **Source E** as evidence of the role of George Washington in the colonists' efforts to attain independence?
   *In reaching a conclusion you should refer to:*
   * *the origin and possible purpose of the source;*
   * *the content of the source;*
   * *recalled knowledge.*    **5**

5. How completely do **Sources C**, **D** and **E** identify the issues affecting the outcome of the War of Independence?
   *Use **Sources C**, **D** and **E** and recalled knowledge.*    **8**

   **(30)**

*[END OF QUESTIONS ON SPECIAL TOPIC 5]*

OPTION C: LATER MODERN HISTORY

SPECIAL TOPIC 6: PATTERNS OF MIGRATION: SCOTLAND 1830s–1930s

**Study the sources below and then answer the questions which follow.**

**Source A:** from the *Glasgow Constitutional,* 4 March 1846.

A mass attack of 300 Irish navvies working ten miles south of Edinburgh, to secure the release of two of their companions who had been imprisoned on suspicion of stealing a watch, led to disastrous consequences for themselves and their families. In demolishing the prison-house and rescuing the prisoners, they came into conflict with the police, one of whom died of injuries received in the scuffle. A detachment of police from Edinburgh imprisoned thirteen of the party, and the Scottish and English labourers on the line who numbered around 2,000, marched to the south end of the line where the Irish navvies were working, set fire to row after row of the Irishmen's huts and beat men, women and children out of the district. An armed body of 200 Irishmen set out from Edinburgh to avenge their countrymen but were turned back by the military.

**Source B:** from *The Scottish Nation*, T. M. Devine, 1999.

The Catholic Irish immigrants were "strangers in a strange land", alien in religion, speech and culture; the scapegoats for every conceivable social ill from drunkenness to the epidemic diseases of the larger towns. In response, the Irish immigrants retreated into themselves, became introverted, pursued a separate identity in Scotland and warmly embraced the Catholic faith which alone provided them with spiritual consolation and a sense of social worth. They could not relate to a Scotland which derived its collective identity from Presbyterianism, a creed which regarded Catholicism as at best a superstitious error and at worst as a satanic force led by the Man of Sin himself, the Pope of Rome. By 1900, the Irish immigrants and their descendants seem to have developed almost as a distinct and introverted ethnic community in Scotland, with its own chapels, schools, social welfare organisations, and political agenda.

**Source C:** from a Census Return, 1871.

This invasion of Irish is likely to produce far more serious effects on the population of Scotland than even the invasions of the warlike Norsemen. The immigration of such a huge number of Irish labourers of the lowest class, with scarcely any education, must have the most prejudicial effects on the Scottish population. It is quite certain that the native Scot who has associated with them has most certainly deteriorated in terms of morals and habits. This very high proportion of the Irish race in Scotland had undoubtedly lowered greatly the moral tone of the lower classes, and greatly increased the need for the enforcement of sanitary and police precautions wherever they are settled in numbers.

**Source D:** from *First Report from the Select Committee on Emigration* (Scotland), 1841.

Nothing tends so much to keep a community of persons going to a strange land together as having someone of superior intelligence, cleverness, and benevolence among them, who being possessed of their confidence and respect, they can look up to as their adviser and friend. Also, by his advice and example he will encourage them to persevere in overcoming difficulties which might be regarded as insurmountable. A clergyman is evidently the person most likely to answer these purposes, and the performance by him of religious services which the emigrants had been accustomed to would, more than anything else, diminish the natural feeling of regret at leaving their native country. Societies and clubs founded by the emigrants also serve to reinforce their identity but it is the role of the clergymen which should not be underestimated.

**Source E:** from *Scots in Canada*, J. Calder (2003).

As Scottish communities became established in Canada, many of them founded St. Andrews, Caledonian and Highland societies, or societies taking their name from a specific Scottish place of origin. A key function of these societies was the support of needy Scots, helping newly-arrived emigrants with cash, information or advice. Commemoration and ritual were also features of these societies' activities, and tartan and music took on a symbolic importance. Even those who felt most positively about their new lives in Canada did not necessarily want to lose their Scottishness.

All this provided an easy and often enjoyable way of maintaining a Scottish identity among immigrants.

[*END OF SOURCES FOR SPECIAL TOPIC 6*]

**SPECIAL TOPIC 6: PATTERNS OF MIGRATION: SCOTLAND 1830s–1930s**

**Answer *all* of the following questions.**

*Marks*

1.  How useful is **Source A** as evidence of the impact of Irish immigration on law and order in Scotland?
    *In reaching a conclusion you should refer to:*
    *   *the origin and possible purpose of the source;*
    *   *the content of the source;*
    *   *recalled knowledge.*                                             5

2.  To what extent did other European immigrants experience similar problems of assimilation as Irish immigrants as identified in **Source B**?
    *Use the source and recalled knowledge.*                             6

3.  How far do **Sources A**, **B** and **C** explain the reasons for anti-Irish feeling among many native Scots?
    *Use **Sources A**, **B** and **C** and recalled knowledge.*        8

4.  Compare the views on Scottish emigrant identity as expressed in **Sources D** and **E.**                                              5
    *Compare the content overall and in detail.*

5.  How fully does **Source E** explain the ways in which Scottish emigrants attempted to maintain their identity in their adopted lands?
    *Use the source and recalled knowledge.*                             6

                                                                         **(30)**

[*END OF QUESTIONS ON SPECIAL TOPIC 6*]

## SPECIAL TOPIC 7:  APPEASEMENT AND THE ROAD TO WAR, TO 1939

**Study the sources below and then answer the questions which follow.**

**Source A:** from the *Daily Sketch*, 9th March (1936).

I should take Hitler at his word.  You cannot for ever keep German troops out of their own territory, and Hitler has now done it without so much as a by-your-leave.  It is a flagrant violation of the Treaty of Versailles, but that treaty is now so tattered as to be unrecognisable.  As it stands, it is impossible to enforce it without war and, as no one wants war, what happens to it is a matter of good manners rather than of good politics.  Unless the powers propose to turn the Germans out, they might as well make a virtue out of necessity and regularise their actions with as much good grace as they command.  There is talk of sanctions through the League of Nations, but sanctions are either a form of sulks or else mean war.

Much the more important question is what Germany plans to do now she has got there.  Herr Hitler offers a twenty-five years Pact of Peace with France and Belgium, and swears by all his gods that he means it.  I believe he does.

**Source B:** from J. Gurney, *Crusade in Spain* (1974).  Gurney was a member of the International Brigade.

The Spanish Civil War seemed to provide the chance for a single individual to take a positive and effective stand on an issue which seemed to be absolutely clear.  Either you were opposed to the growth of fascism and went out to fight against it, or you accepted its crimes, and were guilty of permitting its growth.  There were many people who claimed it was a foreign quarrel, and that nobody other than the Spaniards should involve themselves in it.

But, for myself and many others like me, it was a war of principle, and principles do not have national boundaries.  By fighting against fascism in Spain, we would be fighting against it in our own country and every other.

**Source C:** from the *Aberdeen Press and Journal*, 3rd October, 1938.

In this country, and in many others as well, yesterday was a day of thanksgiving for the avoidance of war. No one who lived through the 1914–1918 struggle, whether facing imminent death in the trenches, or in the nerve-wracked atmosphere at home, could contemplate another war of the same proportions without the deepest horror.  Those who, even yet, are critical of the settlement cannot but join in the universal relief. The dispersal of the war cloud is, above all, the work of the British Prime Minister.  For lives of suffering spared, the horrors of war averted, Europe's thanks are due to him.

**Source D:** from a speech in the House of Commons by Sir Archibald Sinclair, Leader of the Liberal Party, 3rd October, 1938.

A policy which imposes injustices on a small and weak nation, and tyranny on free men and women, can never be the foundation of a lasting peace.  Was it wise for the Prime Minister in his broadcast speech the other night to talk of quarrels in distant lands between peoples of whom we know nothing?  Ought not responsible public men rather strive to make people understand the importance of distant but important places to our lives at home, our standard of living, to the employment of our people and the protection of our liberties?  Czechoslovakia is much nearer home, and my fear is that we shall yet live to regret the day when our government undermined and sacrificed freedom in central Europe, and laid open to the march of Germany all the peoples and resources of Eastern Europe.

**Source E:** from C. Thorne, *The Approach of War* (1968).

Revulsion against war was accompanied by a blend of guilt and idealism for those who felt the principles of lasting peace had been denied to Germany. To appease was to settle just grievance, not to cringe and betray.

The burden of responsibility carried by Chamberlain added negative, practical reasons for the continuing search for a settlement. It was generally accepted, for instance, that in war the bombers would always get through—usually thought of in terms of German bombers over Britain, not vice versa. Those who, at the time, were ready for "peace at any cost in humiliation" may well have been wrong, but they included men of bravery and experience.

*[END OF SOURCES FOR SPECIAL TOPIC 7]*

### SPECIAL TOPIC 7:  APPEASEMENT AND THE ROAD TO WAR, TO 1939

**Answer *all* of the following questions.**

*Marks*

1.  To what extent does **Source A** represent British reaction to the remilitarisation of the Rhineland in March, 1936?
    *Use the source and recalled knowledge.*    **6**

2.  How useful is **Source B** as evidence of the reasons why some British people chose to become involved in the Spanish Civil War?
    *In reaching a conclusion you should refer to:*
    * *the origin and possible purpose of the source;*
    * *the content of the source;*
    * *recalled knowledge.*    **5**

3.  How much support was there at the time for the views expressed in **Source C** towards the Munich Agreement?
    *Use the source and recalled knowledge.*    **6**

4.  Compare the views on the Munich Agreement expressed in **Source C** and **Source D**.
    *Compare the content overall and in detail.*    **5**

5.  How fully do **Sources A**, **C** and **E** explain the reasons for the direction of British foreign policy in the second half of the 1930s?
    *Use **Sources A**, **C** and **E** and recalled knowledge.*    **8**

    **(30)**

*[END OF QUESTIONS ON SPECIAL TOPIC 7]*

## SPECIAL TOPIC 8:  THE ORIGINS AND DEVELOPMENT OF THE COLD WAR 1945–1985

**Study the sources below and then answer the questions which follow.**

**Source A:** from the United States' Note to the USSR on Berlin, August 17, 1961.

On August 13, East German authorities put into effect several measures regulating movement at the boundary of the Western Sectors and the Soviet Sector of the city of Berlin.  The United States Government has never accepted that limitations can be imposed on freedom of movement within Berlin.  The United States Government considers that the measures which the East German authorities have taken are illegal.  The measures which have just been taken are motivated by the fact that an ever increasing number of inhabitants of East Germany wish to leave this territory.  The reasons for this exodus are known.  They are simply the internal difficulties in East Germany.  The United States Government expects the Soviet Government to put an end to these illegal measures.

**Source B:** from the Soviet reply to the United States Note on Berlin, August 18, 1961.

The Soviet Government fully understands and supports the actions of the Government of the German Democratic Republic (GDR) which established effective control on the border with West Berlin.  West Berlin has been transformed into a centre of subversive activity and espionage, into a centre of provocations against the GDR, the Soviet Union, and other socialist countries.  West Berlin authorities did not lift a finger to put an end to this criminal activity.  The Government of the FRG (West Germany) led an army of recruiters who, by means of deception, bribery, and blackmail, encouraged a certain part of the residents of the GDR to migrate to West Berlin.  Thus the protest made in the note of the Government of the USA is without foundation and is rejected by the Soviet Government.

**Source C:** from a Memorandum of October 17, 1962 describing a meeting of President Kennedy with his senior advisers on National Security.

Several alternatives indicated below were considered at the meeting.  All dealt with the specific actions the US Government should take against Cuba at this time.

1.  Do nothing and live with the situation.  It was pointed out clearly that Western Europe, Greece, Turkey and other countries had lived under the Soviet Medium Range Ballistic Missiles (MRBMs) for years.  Therefore, why should the United States be so concerned?

2.  Resort to an all-out blockade which would probably require a declaration of war and would mean the interruption of all incoming shipping.

3.  Military action was considered at several levels:
    (*a*)  attacking identified MRBM installations;
    (*b*)  attacking MRBM installations and airfields with MIG fighters;
    (*c*)  attacking MRBM installations, airfields, surface to air missile sites and coastal missile sites.

Discussions of all of the above were inconclusive.

**Source D:**  from Melvin Small, *Nixon's Flawed Search for Peace*, from *Major Problems in the History of the Vietnam War* (2003).

Nixon knew that it was essential to end the war that had cost the nation so much in human and financial treasure and had led to unprecedented domestic turbulence and the alienation of a good part of the next generation.  He had to end the war as quickly as possible so that he could launch dramatic diplomatic initiatives that, if successful, might avert future Vietnams.

But Nixon was "convinced that how we end this will determine the future of the US in the world".  He had to obtain what he would characterise as "peace with honour"; he could not just "cut and run," leaving the 17 million people of South Vietnam to be taken over by the communist North Vietnamese.

**Source E:** from Walter LaFeber, *America, Russia and the Cold War, 1945–1992* (1993).

The Czechs, during their so-called Prague Spring, even discussed a loosening of their one-party political system. The United States encouraged the process by opening up trade channels. The Brezhnev regime, meanwhile, tightened its control within Russia. Brezhnev warned that dissent could not be tolerated because, "we are living in conditions of an ideological war". Détente meant a lessening of military and political tensions with the West, but ideological coexistence could not be allowed.

The Prague Spring strained this rigid ideological line to the limit. Soviet officials were divided over how to respond. Some Foreign Ministry officials, who did not want to endanger détente, were among those opposing intervention, but they were overbalanced by party leaders who feared ideological and economic contamination from Czech liberalism, and by some military and secret police officials who believed the Czech policies might infect the entire bloc. Brezhnev ordered Soviet troops to smash the Czech regime.

*[END OF SOURCES FOR SPECIAL TOPIC 8]*

### SPECIAL TOPIC 8: THE ORIGINS AND DEVELOPMENT OF THE COLD WAR 1945–1985

**Answer *all* of the following questions.**

*Marks*

1. Compare the views of the Berlin Crisis of 1961 given in **Sources A** and **B**.
   *Compare the content overall and in detail.*

   **5**

2. How useful is **Source B** as evidence of Soviet concerns about Berlin in 1961?
   *In reaching a conclusion you should refer to:*
   • *the origin and possible purpose of the source;*
   • *the content of the source;*
   • *recalled knowledge.*

   **5**

3. To what extent does **Source C** explain the problems faced by the Americans in reacting to the crisis in Cuba?
   *Use the source and recalled knowledge.*

   **6**

4. How fully does **Source D** explain the changes in American policy in Vietnam under President Nixon?
   *Use the source and recalled knowledge.*

   **6**

5. To what extent was ideology the main reason for tension between the Superpowers during the Cold War?
   *Use **Sources B**, **C** and **E** and recalled knowledge.*

   **8**

   **(30)**

*[END OF QUESTIONS ON SPECIAL TOPIC 8]*

### SPECIAL TOPIC 9: IRELAND 1900–1985: A DIVIDED IDENTITY

**Study the sources below and then answer the questions which follow.**

**Source A:** from a speech by Sir Thomas Edmond in the House of Commons, 11 April 1912.

The Irish people have always held that the only power competent to make laws for Ireland is a Parliament of Ireland.

Ireland is anxious to be friends with Britain, provided that Britain shows an anxiety to make friends with her. We Irishmen can honourably accept the Home Rule Bill, with the consent of our people, in the belief that we can work it for the benefit of our country. The whole structure of the Bill itself is an absolute answer to all those who fear that Home Rule means the oppression of the minority or the breaking up of the British Empire. We are quite prepared to join in defending the Empire. Ireland as a free and self-governing nation within the Empire will contribute to its strength and greatness. The majority of the people of Ulster are Home Rulers, although one reason given on the platform for not granting Home Rule is that Ulster is opposed to it. I am satisfied of this, that however much she opposes Home Rule at present, once it is the law of the land, Ulster will accept it and take her part loyally and patriotically in carrying it out.

I do not believe in this division into the north and south of Ireland. I would like to see the Irish question settled with the assistance of Ulster, but if Ulster will not help, it must be settled in spite of her.

**Source B:** from *Ulster's Solemn League and Covenant*, Saturday 28th September 1912.

Being convinced that Home Rule would be disastrous to the well being of Ulster as well as of the whole of Ireland, subversive of our civil and religious freedom, destructive of our citizenship, and perilous to the unity of the Empire, we, men of Ulster, loyal subjects of His Gracious Majesty King George V, do hereby pledge ourselves in Solemn Covenant throughout this our time of threatened calamity to stand by one another in defending ourselves and our children, our cherished position of equal citizenship in the United Kingdom, and in using all means which may be found necessary to defeat the present conspiracy to set up a Home Rule Parliament in Ireland. In the event of such a Parliament being forced upon us we further solemnly pledge ourselves to refuse to recognise its authority. In sure confidence that God will defend the right we hereto subscribe our names.

**Source C:** from Charles Townsend, *Ireland and the Twentieth Century* (1999).

The government's damage limitation exercise was flawed both in conception and in execution. Martial law was seen as a way of encouraging the law abiding majority to support the state. Instead it alienated them. The release of the internees around Christmas 1916 instead of creating gratitude as the government hoped, drove the process on. Collins and his fellow internees had used their time in prisons and camps to lay the foundations for the reorganisation of the national movement. During 1917 Sinn Fein was transformed into a coherent political movement that rapidly picked up support.

Sinn Fein's profile was insistently raised over the summer of 1917. 70 Sinn Fein clubs were formed in the first fortnight of June; the police counted 336 branches by the end of July.

The growth of Sinn Fein as a national movement was made possible by the participation of the Volunteers in politics, and was finally to be cemented by the approval of the Church. The symbolic turning point was the death of Thomas Ashe.

**Source D:** from a speech by Eamon De Valera speaking to the Dail Eireann, December 1921.

We were elected by the Irish people. Did the Irish people think we were liars when we said that we meant to uphold the Republic, which was ratified by the vote of the people three years ago, and was further ratified by the vote of the people at the elections last May?

When the proposal for negotiations came from the British Government asking that we should try by negotiation to reconcile Irish national aspirations with the British Empire, there was no one here as strong as I was to make sure that every human attempt should be made to find whether such reconciliation was possible. I am against this Treaty because it does not reconcile Irish national aspirations with association with the British Government. I am against this Treaty, not because I am a man of war, but a man of peace. I am against this Treaty because it will not end centuries of conflict between Great Britain and Ireland.

We went out to effect such a reconciliation and we have brought back a thing which will not even reconcile our own people, much less reconcile Britain and Ireland.

**Source E:** from *Notes by General Michael Collins*, August 1922.

The Anti Treaty party attempted to stampede meetings by revolver shootings, to wreck trains, the suppression of free speech, of the liberty of the press, terrorisation and sabotage of a kind that we were familiar with a year ago. And with what object? With the sole object of preventing the people from expressing their will, and of making the government of Ireland by the representatives of the people as impossible as the British government was made impossible by the united forces a year ago.

Their policy had now become clear—to prevent the people's will being carried out because it differed from their own, to create trouble in order to break up the only possible national government, and to destroy the Treaty with utter recklessness as to the consequences.

[*END OF SOURCES FOR SPECIAL TOPIC 9*]

## SPECIAL TOPIC 9:  IRELAND 1900–1985:  A DIVIDED IDENTITY

**Answer *all* of the following questions.**

*Marks*

1.  How typical is the attitude expressed in **Source A** of Irish attitudes to Home Rule?
    *Use the source and recalled knowledge.*    **6**

2.  Compare the views expressed in **Sources A** and **B** towards Home Rule.
    *Compare the content overall and in detail.*    **5**

3.  To what extent does **Source C** explain why Sinn Fein gained victory in the election of 1918?
    *Use the source and recalled knowledge.*    **6**

4.  How useful is **Source D** as evidence of Irish attitudes to the Anglo Irish Treaty?
    *In reaching a conclusion you should refer to:*
    *  *the origin and possible purpose of the source;*
    *  *the content of the source;*
    *  *recalled knowledge.*    **5**

5.  How fully do **Sources B**, **D** and **E** explain the causes of division and conflict in Ireland during the period 1912–1922?
    *Use **Sources B**, **D** and **E** and recalled knowledge.*    **8**

**(30)**

[*END OF QUESTIONS ON SPECIAL TOPIC 9*]

[*END OF QUESTION PAPER*]

[BLANK PAGE]

[BLANK PAGE]

[BLANK PAGE]

[BLANK PAGE]

# Acknowledgements

Permission has been sought from all relevant copyright holders and Bright Red Publishing is grateful for the use of the following:

**2006 Paper**
Detail from the Bayeux Tapestry. Reproduced by special permission of the City of Bayeux (p 4); An extract from 'The Norman Conquest' by HR Loyn published by Hutchinson © Cengage Learning Services Limited (p 5); An extract from 'William The Conqueror' (1989) by D Bates, published by Tempus. Reproduced by permission of The History Press (p 5); An illumination from the thirteenth-century manuscript, 'Les Histoires d'Outremer' © Bibliothèque nationale de France (p 6); An extract from 'Essential Histories #1 The Crusades' by David Nicolle (2001) © Osprey Publishing (p 7); An extract from 'Crusade' by Terry Jones and Alan Ereira, published by BBC Books 1996. Reprinted by permission of The Random House Group (p 7); An extract from 'The Union of Scotland and England' by PWJ Riley (1978), © PWJ Riley (p 8); An extract from 'The New Penguin History of Scotland: From the Earliest Times to the Present Day', edited by RA Houston and WWJ Knox (Allen Lane and the Penguin Press 2001, Penguin Books 2002). Editorial and introductory material copyright © R.A. Houston and W.W.J. Knox, 2001. Reproduced by permission Penguin Books Ltd (p 8); An extract from 'Slavery, Abolition and Emancipation: Volume 2 – The Abolition Debate' by Peter J Kitson, reproduced with the permission of Pickering & Chatto Publishers (p 10); An extract from 'Abolitionists Black and White' by Adrian Hastings, taken from 'The Atlantic Slave Trade' edited by D Northrup (2002) published by Houghton Mifflin Co. (p 11); An extract from 'The War for Independence, to Saratoga' by D Higginbotham, taken from 'A Companion to the American Revolution' edited by J Greene and R Pole, published by Blackwells, 2000 (p 12); An extract from 'The Irish in the Victorian City' by R Swift and S Gilley (1985), published by Routledge © Taylor & Francis Group (p 14); An extract from 'Scotland's Story', © STV, 1988 (p 15); An extract from a speech by Winston Churchill in the House of Commons, 19th July 1937. Parliamentary material is reproduced with the permission of the Controller of HMSO on behalf of Parliament (p 16); An extract from 'Appeasement' published by HarperCollins Publishers Ltd © 1998 Andrew Boxer (p 16); An extract from a speech by Viscount Astor in Parliament, 16 March 1938. Parliamentary material is reproduced with the permission of the Controller of HMSO on behalf of Parliament (p 16); The cover of the magazine 'Illustrazione del Popolo', 9–15 October 1938 © Mary Evans Picture Library (p 17); An extract from 'The Twentieth Century World' (4th Edition, 2001) by WR Keylor. Reproduced by permission of Oxford University Press, Inc (p 18); An extract from 'US Foreign Policy Since 1945' by Dobson and Marsh (2001), published by Routledge © Taylor & Francis Group (p 18); An extract from a speech by John Redmond in The House of Commons, 15 September 1914. Parliamentary material is reproduced with the permission of the Controller of HMSO on behalf of Parliament (p 20); An extract from 'The Rising and After' by FSL Lyons, taken from 'A New History of Ireland', edited by WE Vaughan (1996). By permission of Oxford University Press (p 20); An extract from an article in 'The Irish Times' 1st May 1916 © The Irish Times (p 20); An extract from 'Britain and Ireland: From Home Rule to Independence' by Jeremy Smith (2000). Reproduced by permission of Pearson Education (p 21).

**2007 Paper**
An extract from 'The Battle of Hastings' by Jim Bradbury, (1998), published by Sutton. Reproduced by permission of The History Press (p 4); An extract from 'Scotland: A History' by Fiona Watson, (2001), published by Tempus. Reproduced by permission of The History Press (p 5); The picture, 'Peter the Hermit leads the People's Crusades' (British Library Record No: 2095, Shelfmark: Egerton 1500, P Folio No: f.45v). Reproduced with permission of The British Library (p 6); An extract from 'The Crusades' by Zoë Oldenbourg, published by Weidenfield and Nicolson, an imprint of the Orion Publishing Group, London (p 7); An extract from 'God Wills It' by WB Bartlett (1999), published by Sutton. Reproduced by permission of The History Press (p 7); An extract from 'Image and Identity' by Broun, Finlay & Lynch (eds), reproduced by permission of John Donald, an imprint of Birlinn Ltd www.birlinn.co.uk (p 8); An extract from 'Kingdom or Province? Scotland and the Regal Union' by Keith Brown, (1992), published by Macmillan Educational Ltd © Keith Brown (p 8); An extract from 'Thomas Clarkson' by Earl Leslie Griggs, (1936), published by Allen & Unwin. Public Domain (p 10); An extract from 'Slavery, Industrialisation and Abolition' by Eric Williams, in D Northrup (ed), 'The Atlantic Slave Trade' (2002), published by Houghton Mifflin Co. (p 10); An extract from 'The Slave Trade' by Hugh Thomas, (1997), published by Simon & Schuster © Hugh Thomas (p 11); An extract from 'The American Revolution: An Eyewitness History' by David F Burg, (2001) published by Facts on File (p 12); An extract from 'Revolution in America: Britain and the Colonies, 1763–1776' by Peter DG Thomas © University of Wales Press (p 12); An extract from 'Ayr Advertiser', 1849 © Ayr Advertiser (p 14); Extract from 'Scotland, Sectarianism, and the Irish diaspora', by Danny McGowan, in Frontline Online (p 14); An extract from 'Scots in Canada' by Jenni Calder, published by Luath Press (p 15); A cartoon by David Low from 1938 'He only wants to lie down with your lamb' © Solo Syndication/Associated Newspapers Ltd (p 16); A letter by Douglas Reed, foreign correspondent of The Times to his editor © The Times/NI Syndication, March 1938 (p 16); An extract from 'Making Friends with Hitler' by Ian Kershaw, (Penguin Books, 2004). Copyright © Ian Kershaw, 2004.